Author's route
→ by air
·········· by road

MW00450597

CHINA

NORTH VIETNAM

•HANOI

LAOS

•Vinh

Gulf
of
Tonkin

DMZ (Demilitarized Zone)
— *Ben Hai River*
• Dong Ha

• Hue

Hainan Dao

LAOS

• Da Nang

VIETNAM

Plei Beng

• Quang Ngai

Pleiku

N

• Qui Nhon

200 MILES
scale decreases with perspective

INA SEA

GHOSTS OF WAR

GHOSTS OF WAR

Chasing My Father's Legend
Through Vietnam

ERIC REGULY

sh.

**SUTHERLAND
HOUSE**

TORONTO, 2022

Sutherland House
416 Moore Ave., Suite 205
Toronto, ON M4G 1C9

Copyright © 2022 by Eric Reguly

First edition, April 2022

If you are interested in inviting one of our authors to a live event or
media appearance, please contact matt@sutherlandhousebooks.com
and visit our website at sutherlandhousebooks.com for more
information about our authors and their schedules.

Manufactured in Canada
Cover designed by Lena Yang
Book composed by Karl Hunt

Library and Archives Canada Cataloguing in Publication
Title: Ghosts of war : chasing my father's legend through Vietnam / Eric Reguly.
Names: Reguly, Eric, author.
Identifiers: Canadiana 20210370637 | ISBN 9781989555606 (hardcover)
Subjects: LCSH: Reguly, Eric—Travel—Vietnam. | LCSH: Foreign correspondents—
Canada—Biography. | LCSH: Fathers and sons—Canada—Biography. | LCSH: Foreign
correspondents—Travel—Vietnam. | LCSH: Vietnam War, 1961-1975—Press coverage. |
LCSH: Vietnam—Description and travel. | LCGFT: Autobiographies.
Classification: LCC PN4913.R45 A3 2022 | DDC 070.4/332092—dc23

ISBN 978-1-989555-60-6

CONTENTS

For my mother Ada and my sisters Susan and Rebecca.
Bob's journey was theirs too.

PRELUDE

CHEVY CHASE, MARYLAND. Summer, 1967—It is early one morning in late July. I am nine years old and excited to see Dad, who has just returned from almost three months in Vietnam. I creep into the bedroom and leap onto his chest, expecting him to laugh and hug me.

In an instant, I am flying backward, gasping, clutching my chest.

He didn't mean to punch me. He was still in his foxhole.

CHAPTER 1

The Things He Carried

ROME, JANUARY 2018—Finally, the big day had come. I was packing for my flight to Ho Chi Minh City, still better known as Saigon. Even before the death of my eighty-year-old father, Robert Reguly, in 2011, I had dreamt of retracing his steps during the Vietnam War, which he covered for the *Toronto Star* when he was thirty-six years old, at the peak of his career. At the time, he was the *Star's* Washington bureau chief and Canada's most famous print journalist.

Three precious objects in my home office in Rome demanded my attention as I filled my bags. The first was the German-built Olympia portable typewriter that Dad, known as 'Bob' to his family and friends, lugged around Vietnam. It had a couple of dents but worked perfectly. The second was a brick-heavy Nikkormat camera, black, one of two he used as a foreign correspondent in the United States, Indochina, the Middle East, Africa, and the Indian Subcontinent. It, too, worked perfectly. The third was a US Army knapsack, complete with insulated green plastic water bottles that he bought on the black market the day after he arrived in Saigon in May 1967 and carried into war.

For a moment I toyed with an idea. Why not take pictures in Vietnam with his camera, write on his Olympia, and traipse across former battle zones with his knapsack? How romantic.

In the end, none of the three made the cut. Looking at my map of Vietnam, now splattered with pink dots, each marking a spot he had visited (or close enough), I realized I would be on the move constantly, without the benefit of a Huey helicopter. Best to travel light, as he did. I am sure he left his typewriter at a US Marine or Army base before he went into combat areas.

What did make it into my bags, other than the requisite *Dispatches*, a book on the war by *Esquire* magazine writer Michael Herr, were copies of the original stories Dad banged out in Vietnam, retrieved from a musty filing cabinet in my mother's Toronto basement. Their place lines—Saigon, Pleiku, Hue, DMZ, Plei Beng and others—would be my compass. I had grown up hearing these names over and over, but I never knew where they were, or what precisely happened in them. I was not even sure they all still existed. Would they now be covered by forest, highways, or malls, or seared into what seemed moonscape by bombs and Agent Orange?

What I did know was that these spots forever changed my father and, by extension, his family—especially me, his oldest child and only son.

When I was young, I saw my father as a heroic, glamorous, semi-mythical figure, even if I suspected, by then, that he was not a model father or husband. Dad was always travelling, always working, forever dashing off on dangerous assignments. I remember him taking me to early morning hockey practice but I do not remember him coming to a single event at school: no parent-teacher meetings, no concerts. At the time, his absences did not bother me. I did not know any better. Years later, with children of my own, I would realize that his physical and psychological absence was the root of the everlasting damage he inflicted on the family. A decade after his death, the surviving Regulys still carried the scars of an absentee father and husband. My storybook hero was gone.

But when I was a kid, all I saw was a hard-living daredevil with a typewriter. And I wanted to be just like him. While I would never become a "bang-bang" correspondent, to use the journalist argot for war reporter, our careers would have a few notable similarities. I am based in Rome for *The Globe and Mail*, covering Europe, North Africa, and the Middle East. My father was based in Rome for the *Toronto Star* from 1969 through 1972, covering the same territory, and beyond. We both had US postings—Dad in Washington, DC, me in New York—and long stints as investigative reporters.

I would be lying if I said I had not felt competitive with him over the years. When he praised my stories, my spirits would soar. When he thought they were lame, naïve, or insufficiently critical of power in any form, my heart would sink. "Beneath your veneer," he would sometimes say, laughing, "there's more veneer."

Or, again laughing: "Eric, there's less to you than meets the eye."

Still, I know he was proud of my career as journalist, even if he never told me that directly. I know because my mother, Ada, told me. Dad was from that generation of men who found it unmanly to express or display emotion. I can't remember him once telling me that he loved me, even if I knew he did. I loved him intensely, though I knew it embarrassed him when I told him that. He was my guiding light.

Through Dad, I became aware of the world. Through him, I experienced the Vietnam War vicariously, wishing I had been born twenty years earlier so I, too, could have jumped on Hueys as if they were taxis to skim over the lush Vietnamese forest on the way to a battle, and back to Saigon in time for martinis.

It's not that I have a taste for gore. In my mind, and my father's, the Vietnam War was the biggest event of its era. If you were a journalist and didn't go to "Nam," you missed out on one of America's greatest and most tragic geopolitical sagas, a national wound that has yet to heal.

Even though my father returned from Vietnam skinny, wild-eyed, and taut as a guitar string, the war did not seem to zap him with a heavy dose of post-traumatic stress disorder (PTSD), a condition known as shell shock in that era. My mother said that the destruction and bloodshed he witnessed did not disturb him terribly, but I think she was partly wrong. Again, men of his era hid their emotions. He may not have had the shakes, the pounding heart, or the nausea, but I suspect he suffered other symptoms including anxiety and vivid nightmares. If he did, he certainly would not have told us because doing so would have been, in his view, a sign of weakness. I believe that, like many of his war correspondent friends, he dealt with the feelings and flashbacks by self-medicating with copious amounts of alcohol, nicotine, and womanizing, and by denying he was anything but invincible. Dad and his colleagues were young, brawny men when they covered the war. More than a few of them later fell apart, lost in a sea of alcohol, broken marriages, and tortured relationships with their editors and colleagues. I am aware of at least one of my father's war correspondent buddies who committed suicide, and others who died young. Still others turned into war junkies, bored with normal life and unwilling or unable to adapt to it. Dad became less attentive as a father, maybe because his brain was zapped by so many images of violent death, maybe because he was consciously or subconsciously yearning to recapture the excitement and purpose that propelled him through his months in an all-out war zone in what was the biggest story on the planet.

He certainly became more cynical, more skeptical of American foreign policy, and leaned more to the political left. Dad loved covering the war but hated it at the same time. He thought it was unwinnable, morally unjust, and completely unnecessary—a war of choice against a country that posed no threat to the United States. He knew that ferocious American firepower was killing a lot of innocent Vietnamese peasants. From that point on, he never considered American foreign policy a force of good, not in Southeast Asia, not in the Middle East, not in Africa.

My goal in retracing his footsteps in Vietnam was to learn more about how he covered the war, what motivated him, and how it changed him. Was he just an adrenaline junkie with a typewriter, or was his motivation less selfish? Why did the war mean so much to him, and why did he choose to live the way he lived?

One other thing. My father thought he killed a man, or men. Journalists are not supposed to do that. I wanted to find the spot where a Marine handed him an M16 automatic rifle at the start of a vicious firefight and told Dad he was on his own. The casualties were piling up. It was every man for himself. When Dad pulled the trigger, was he a journalist or a warrior? Maybe my journey would help me answer that question, too. So off I went to Vietnam, half a century after he went, with absolutely no idea what I would discover.

CHAPTER 2

The Boy with One Eye

FORT WILLIAM, ONTARIO, 1931 and Vancouver, British Columbia, 1958—Bob Reguly was given the *Toronto Star*'s Washington, DC posting in the summer of 1966, a reward for having won two National Newspaper Awards (NNAs) for investigative journalism.[1] The first of these distinguished awards came in 1964 for his work tracking down a notorious fugitive from Canadian justice, the mobbed-up union leader, Hal Banks, who had skipped bail on assault charges in Montreal and disappeared. Even the Federal Bureau of Investigation (FBI) and the Royal Canadian Mounted Police (RCMP) couldn't find him. My father discovered him living on a yacht in Flatbush, Brooklyn.

Two years later, a headline blared "Star Man Finds Gerda Munsinger." An East German prostitute and probable Soviet agent, Munsinger had had an affair with Pierre Sévigny, a cabinet minister in the government of Prime Minister John Diefenbaker in the late 1950s. Although she was said to be dead, my father found her very much alive in Munich. When he banged on her door, she thought he was an assassin sent to silence her.

---

1   In 1968, he would win a third for a series on racism in America. I was the co-winner of an NNA in 2010 in the less glamorous business writing category.

Dad was six-foot-two, brawny, strong-jawed, and dark-haired, with an Elvis Presley haircut, the picture of virility. His big, easy grin belied his toughness. His achievements were all the more remarkable when you consider his childhood, which was miserable and deprived even by the standards of the Great Depression. He was born on January 19, 1931 in the east end (the wrong end) of Fort William (now Thunder Bay), Ontario, a small cultural melting pot of Poles, Finns, Italians, Ukrainians, and Slovaks. Slovak was his first language and the one he used as an adult to speak to his parents.

With a population today of 110,000, Thunder Bay lies on the northwest shore of Lake Superior, about 1,400 kilometres north-west of Toronto by car. In my father's day, Thunder Bay was made up of two adjacent cities, Fort William and Port Arthur, which amalgamated in 1970. The city is surrounded by vast tracts of wilderness. It has long, frigid winters and short, delightful summers that attract outdoor adventurers from southern Ontario, Minnesota, and Wisconsin, plus a few wilderness enthusiasts from Europe. In 1968, Dad bought an acre of virgin waterfront land for C$400 on Lac des Mille Lacs, a big, backwoods lake about ninety minutes by car west of Thunder Bay. He built a cedar cottage on it. For some forty years, the cottage was my father's labour of love, and ours, too We cleared the land together, rock by rock. And every summer we spent weeks fighting over which trees to cut down, and repairing the damage caused by ice.

Once in a while, when I am in Thunder Bay with my family to load up with food and other supplies for the cottage, we drive by Dad's childhood home at 305 Robertson Street. Today, as then, the house is an unremarkable wood-sided bungalow. Tiny, not much more than a shack, though one with an impeccably maintained garden. It is where my father's parents, Josef and Maria, raised seven children after they emigrated from Czechoslovakia. We can't imagine how they all fitted.

It's also hard to imagine how Dad went from such humble beginnings to travel the world, hobnobbing with the famous and infamous. Like most of his friends and relatives, he could have dropped out of high school, worked in a sawmill or grain elevator, found solace in booze, fishing, and hockey, married the girl next door and lived a fairly comfortable, lower middle-class life in a city whose main links to the outside world were the grain ships that arrived from the St. Lawrence River to fill their cargo holds with Prairie durum wheat. Instead, he ended up in the jungles of Vietnam and on the US campaign trail, chasing Bobby Kennedy and Richard Nixon. And when he wasn't doing that, he was hunting spies.

* * *

My grandfather and grandmother, Josef Reguly and Maria Lehocky, were from the Slovak side of what was then Czechoslovakia, in nearby towns in the Tatra Mountains, just south of the Polish border. Maria, born in 1894, was an only child. She was sent to Canada at the age of fifteen after her father was killed. He fell under his farm wagon while trying to rein in a pair of runaway horses. Maria never saw her mother again. She met my grandfather in Thunder Bay and they were married in the local Slovak Catholic church, St. Peter's, on January 13, 1913. She was nineteen. He was twenty-four.

Josef's father, Josef Sr., my great-grandfather, immigrated to Canada in 1898. He worked for five years blasting a rail line through the Crow's Nest Pass in the Rocky Mountains and saved enough money to bring his wife and four children to Canada. In 1903, he boarded a ship to England to pick them up. He died of an unknown fever on the way and was buried in Liverpool, probably in an unmarked grave (I have never tried to find it). His widow, unable to support her two sons and two daughters, sent them to Canada to live with relatives. They arrived in Fort William in 1905. Already it was a rough industrial and rail town whose main activity was loading grain, and for decades it would be the world's largest inland port. Pulp and paper plants, a shipyard, and, later, a factory for the construction of war-planes, including the Hawker Hurricane—the star of the Battle of Britain in 1940—were significant sideshows. Dad remembers working in the aircraft factory near the end of the war, when he was thirteen or fourteen, stacking aluminum sheets that would be used to make the Curtiss SB2C Helldiver dive bombers used by the Americans in the Pacific. He had a fascination with aircraft even as a kid and working in a warplane factory must have been a dream come true.

Josef Jr., my father's father, drove a truck for the Swift Canadian Company, a meat processor, delivering sides of beef to butchers. He was issued Province of Ontario driver's licence No. 19, making him one of the few drivers in northwestern Ontario and a real curiosity in an era when horses filled the streets. He smoked a pipe and White Owl cigars, but not cigarettes, and the family vehicle was the very truck he drove at Swift, which he purchased after he quit the company to work on the farm he had bought. The truck was a 1913 REO with wooden-spoke wheels and chain drive. It would be worth a fortune today but he traded it for a keg of beer just after the Second World War, when he unloaded the farm, having decided it was too much work. My father remembers playing on the massive old machine as a child.

Josef Jr. spent most of his post-farming career doing various jobs in the grain elevators, where seventy-two-hour weeks were normal. By all accounts, he was immensely strong. Dad said his father could toss one-hundred-pound sacks of wheat when he was seventy-five. (My father was strong too, even well into his sixties, in spite of having undergone qua-druple bypass heart surgery when he was in his mid-fifties.) Until late in life, Josef Jr. rode around town on an ancient Massey-Harris bicycle. He died at eighty-nine. The official cause of death was pneumonia, although he suffered from prostate cancer and psoriasis in his late years. I remember the old man and his halting English fairly well, but never found him especially genial and my mother never liked him. She said he treated his wife like a work animal. Dad was much closer to his mother, Maria. She called him "my Bobby" or "my little Bobby."

Josef Jr. and Maria raised six natural children—Edward, the eldest, Sophie, Mary, Appolonia (known as Apples), Charles, and Robert—and formally adopted Sophie's daughter, Joan, who was born to an unknown father. My father was the youngest of the natural children. They grew up physically close in that tiny bungalow on Robertson Street. I remember my father telling me that he and his brothers shared a single large bed, sleep-ing head to toe, marking out their individual space with strings stretched from headboard to footboard. Any limb that accidently crossed the string boundary in the night would be met with an immediate thump.

All the Reguly siblings, except my father, lived out their entire lives in or near Thunder Bay. His sister Mary was the family's tragedy. She died from a botched illegal abortion when she was seventeen. Charlie was Dad's favourite. He was six years older than my father, a star hockey player who played one professional game with the Toronto Maple Leafs before being snatched up by the Second World War in 1944, although he never made it overseas. Charlie spent his career as a grain inspector and drove a sporty black 1967 Ford Mustang, a car I coveted and wanted to buy from him when I was in my late teens and a frequent visitor to his cluttered home. Dad was distraught when Charlie, a bachelor, died of a burst aneurysm in his early sixties in the cheap bungalow their parents had lived in during their senior years. He was alone in the house and his body was not found until several days after his death.

About a year before Dad died, he wrote a short family history that captured the hardship, especially for his mother, Maria, of growing up poor in the Great Depression:

> Maria gradually expired from a lifetime of overwork—seven children to raise, no hot water, scrub board instead of a washing machine, a wood-burning stove. Winters were long and cold inside as well as out. But the family never lacked for food; they raised chickens, turnips, beets, tons of potatoes, hundreds of lake herring smoked in a backyard apple-wood smoker and two backyard pigs dispatched at Christmas time. All this in a two-bedroom wooden home with no basement.

When I think of Dad, I think of potatoes. He was raised on them, loved them, and always made sure our house was full of them, even if half would go uneaten. Stocking up on staples was part of the Depression-era mentality that never left him. In his mind, hoarding food must have been a way of minimizing risk, which I always found peculiar, given that playing it safe was the least of his goals in his professional life.

Maria died of diabetes at the age of seventy-nine in the autumn of 1972, a few weeks after my father moved us back to Toronto from Rome. He did not get to Thunder Bay in time to say goodbye to her. Her last words, according to one of his siblings who was at her hospital bedside, were, "My Bobby, I want to see my Bobby." The only time in my life I saw Dad cry, other than tearing up during a particularly soppy Three Tenors opera, was when he learned his mother was gone. He hung up the phone, stumbled over to the kitchen table, sat down and wailed in grief. He was forty-one years old. I was in my early teens, and shocked to see that my superman father was human after all.

The wretchedness the Regulys endured in the 1930s and 1940s does not really explain what motivated Dad to escape Thunder Bay and make a name for himself in a career alien to his parents and siblings. I have a couple of theories. The not-so-serious one is that he inherited some of his father's rebel DNA. Shortly after Josef Jr. reached North America, he worked in the Pennsylvania coal mines. He was still a teenager. His job was to lead pit ponies that hauled coal wagons to the elevator shaft. When a strike was called, he was nominated to blow up a coal-gas pipeline, which he did, making him a terrorist of sorts. Pursued by Pinkerton detectives, he fled to Canada and landed in Fort William, which was then the largest Slovak community in Canada.

My more serious theory is that reading broadened my father's horizons and expanded his dreams. As a child, he was a social outcast. When he was five years old, another kid accidentally shot an arrow into his left eye, displacing the pupil and essentially rendering the eye useless. He could only see shadows with it. That wasn't the problem. The problem was that a scab, in the form of an opaque whiteish film, formed over the eye, giving him a freakish appearance even though he was an otherwise strapping, handsome lad. Dad told me that had his parents known enough to take him to a hospital immediately, the eye could have been partly or largely repaired. But they had no money and socialized medicine did not exist in Ontario in the 1930s. Dad went into self-imposed exile and read, developing a passion for literature, satire, adventures, and political and historical treatises. These books opened the world to him from his cramped, cold hovel on Robertson Street.

My bookshelf is still filled with books that Dad bought or recommended: Joseph Conrad, S. J. Perelman, Peter De Vries, Graham Greene,

Ernest Hemingway, John Steinbeck, Robert Louis Stevenson, Jack Kerouac, Raymond Chandler, H. L. Mencken, Joseph Heller, and the author of *Beau Geste,* P. C. Wren. He passed on his love of literature to his children. He studied English literature at university, as did I.

Pulp fiction enraged him. "Life's too short for bad books," he would tell us. I remember him ripping a blatantly commercial romantic novel out of my hands when I was in high school and flinging it into the garbage. He read books even when he was on dangerous assignments. My mother would find the back half of paperbacks in his luggage when she was unpacking it after he returned from trips; he would read the first half of a book, then rip it down the spine and throw it away to save space and weight. "Always travel light," he would tell me when I, too, hit the road as a journalist. It was good advice: foreign correspondents often have to jump onto a plane or train at a moment's notice.

He was a smart kid. The late Charles "Jim" Eccles, a childhood friend who was born two days before Dad and attended the same Fort William Catholic elementary school, St. Stanislaus, told me after Dad died that "Bob and I were often at the head of the class. One semester it would be Bob, the next myself. We kept this up throughout our elementary years."

His love for reading clearly triggered a lust for adventure and helped him escape the mundane existence that seemed mapped out for him. His first paying summer job, when he in his late teens, was in the wilds of northern Ontario. He worked as a timber scaler. Using a canoe that would be dropped into remote areas by a float plane, the job required a small team of men to map out stretches of forest that would be cut by the forestry companies. On those trips, he and his crew had to be entirely self-sufficient. They would catch fish for dinner, drink lake water, and cut tree branches to make frames for their canvas tents, which had no floors. They would sleep on the ground.

His love of literature expanded his horizons academically, too. He attended the University of Western Ontario, half way between Toronto and Detroit, the first in his family to make it beyond high school. A poor student wanting to earn beer money, he joined a parachute club at nearby Kitchener Airport and became a stunt jumper. He was a maniac. He did free-fall jumps, not the much safer static-line jumps, where a cord automatically deploys the parachute a moment after the jumper leaves the plane. He did them so he could dazzle the audience by opening his chute as low as possible.

The free-falls weren't the acts of a natural showman: Dad was quite awkward in front on an audience of more than four or five. He was an adrenaline junkie, and also courageous. Dangerous situations didn't hold him back; they lured him. My sister, Susan, the middle sibling who works as a teacher in Toronto, thinks arrogance also played a role. He thought he was invincible, even in his final years, when he would resist hospital treatment as his heart failed and his lungs filled with liquid. "He never believed death would come knocking for him," she told me. "Yes, he was brave, but Dad also had a great capacity for denial, that nothing would take him down, even when he was at home, dying."

One of my most prized possessions is a logbook of his jumps from 1953 and 1954, when he was in his early twenties. The book gives basic information for each jump, altitude, plane, pilot, and parachute diameter, with a short space to describe the "operation." On May 1, 1954, at the Kitchener Air Show, he jumped out of a tiny Fleet 80 Canuck airplane from 2,600 feet, with a pilot named Shorty at the controls. His tiny, neat handwriting told a harrowing story in a dozen words. "Free-fall, 25 mph wind, hit runway, dragged over ½ mile, out cold, hospital."

Less than three weeks later, he had another close call: "Delay, opened reserve [chute], couldn't find main chute rip cord, opened [at] 200 feet. Close."

By "close" he meant that if his chute had opened a millisecond later, he would have slammed into the ground and shattered every bone in his body and died. He told me that he hit with such force that everyone watching him was sure he was finished. But he didn't break a single bone, a measure of his strength.

Dad never forgot how to do high-speed impact parachute rolls. One summer at our family cottage, he fell off the roof, where he was fixing shingles, twice in one day from a fair height. Each time, his old instincts took over. He rolled and clambered back to his feet while his children and our mother watched in alarm from the porch, sure that he had broken his ankles or legs. He was seventy-seven years old. "Never felt better," he said, grinning.

His stunt jumps and thirst for adventure led to the greatest summer job of all time. In the spring of 1953, he joined the Saskatchewan Smokejumpers, a madcap group of thrill seekers who would parachute into fires to put them out. The now-legendary Smokejumpers were formed by the Saskatchewan Department of Natural Resources in 1947 and based in La Ronge, an old fur-trading post about 400 kilometres north of Saskatoon, one of the province's two main cities. Back then, there were no helicopters and no water bombers to reach forest fires. The Smokejumpers would parachute into burning wilderness that was too far from water to land a float plane. They would snuff out the fire with water pumps or redirect it away from inhabited areas by digging trenches that acted as fire breaks. Completely exhausted after putting out the fire, they would trudge their way through the forest to the nearest lake, where they would be picked up by a float plane, usually a Noorduyn Norseman.

The Smokejumpers were made up of eight-man crews, each member as fit as a Navy Seal. Vintage black and white film shows them training by jumping off the backs of half-ton trucks weaving along dirt roads, and doing tethered jumps off steel towers. Writing about the Smokejumpers in 1956, Dennis Kelly, a war-time paratrooper instructor who became the unit's first jumpmaster, said the training was deliberately gruelling: "By the end of the first week, they have to be able to run six miles [ten kilometres] and at the end of the second, tumble safely from the back of a truck traveling at 30 mph [50 kph]." Dad was shocked, at first, by the physical demands. "I thought I was fit when I arrived but I crawled to bed for the first week, too tired to eat supper," he wrote in a story published in 1997 in the Saskatoon *StarPhoenix*. The job paid $7.76 a day, less $1.50 for board.

When the Smokejumpers were scrambled to fight fires, they carried forty to one hundred pounds of equipment, including water, first-aid kits, shovels, Pulaski tools (a combination of axe and adze), mosquito repellent, lights, maps, and a bedroll in case they had to muck in overnight. They would slide through a short tube mounted in the belly of Norseman planes and drop between the two floats, "like plunging through a hangman's trapdoor," he wrote. The work was incredibly dangerous. Dad would recall almost with glee how crown fires galloped through the canopies of trees faster than a man could run "and had the roaring sound of a giant blowtorch." Superheated trees would explode around him as their sap ignited. But the Saskatchewan Smokejumpers never lost a man in their twenty-year history, unlike some of their American counterparts, who died when the wind and the fire suddenly turned against them. His logbook mentions men getting blown into lakes, tangled in trees and barely missing high-tension electrical wire on training jumps.

Recalling his colleagues, he wrote:

> It was a unit that attracted adventurers; they were very fit and so, naturally enough, they considered themselves indestructible.
>
> Another requirement was that they had to be "temperamentally stable." I guess that meant we all had to have a screw loose, and maybe it was a subliminal requirement for the job.
>
> They had the special swagger of cocky guys who knew with supreme confidence that they were the best at their job. Yes, they scorned macho posturing: after all, arriving by parachute was simply a way of commuting to work. The real work began when they landed.

Describing one operation, he wrote:

> We landed right beside the fire and worked all night and the next day, managing to turn it so that it burned back on itself . . . In the evening we received a hurry-up call that a fire was sweeping down on a drilling camp a few miles away. We were picked up by a motorboat and spent the night throwing burning embers out of the fuel dump with gloved hands as the fire crowned and, luckily, roared past, hurling burning chunks of wood a half kilometre.

If my father was ever genuinely happy—he had a miserable childhood, a troubled marriage, and long bouts of quiet-but-wretched despondency after a libel case went against him when he was in his early fifties—it was during those two summers in La Ronge, especially the summer of 1953, when the fires were particularly frequent and fierce, sometimes requiring two jumps a day. He was dashing and tall, with thick dark hair and green eyes. By then, the scab had been removed from his left eye and it looked almost normal. By all accounts, he was popular with his crew, loved to drink and smoke, loved to fight, and loved his Smokejumper buddies, hard, honest, brave men who he would talk about with admiration decades later, as if they were blood brothers. He said he would have defended them to the death. "Looking back, it was the best time in our lives," he said in the *StarPhoenix*.

Although the scab was gone from his eye by the time he was a Smokejumper, he was still almost totally blind on that side, which may have saved him from a life in the middle of nowhere. He loved airplanes and the outdoors and might have been a bush pilot if he had maintained full vision.[2]

* * *

There is little doubt that Dad's zeal for adventure, and his ability to string sentences together with economy and flair, the by-product of all those years with his nose in a book, prompted Dad's lunge into journalism. If he considered other careers, I don't know of them.

But journalism wasn't the only thing on his mind. Shortly before he graduated from Western in 1953, he was set up on a blind date in Toronto with a woman who had run away from her home in Sudbury, northern

---

2   Me? I never had the guts to jump out of planes, although I had dangerous jobs after high school, including working in an underground mine in northern Manitoba, and an open-pit mine in northwestern Ontario. I also drove enormous tractor-trailer trucks to earn money for university. But I did follow in my father's academic footsteps. I also went to the University of Western Ontario to study literature, mostly for convenience, not to emulate him; it was close to home. And for a year or so his old parachute, a surplus silk one from the Second World War, was pinned to the ceiling of the front room of my campus apartment, turning it into a ridiculous white cave that did not endear me to the girls I brought home. I put it up partly out of sentiment. I can't remember what happened to it after I left university. I doubt I would have discarded such a precious heirloom.

Ontario, so she could finish the high-school education that her parents did not want her to have, and start a career. The woman was Ada Mafalda Baldassi, then no more than nineteen years old. Ada was tall for an Italian woman, five-foot-eight, slim and darkly pretty, with black hair that carried a hint of auburn. She spoke English and Italian and, although she had little money, dressed and ate well. She must have seemed a totally exotic creature to my smart but near-bumpkin father, who was raised on cabbage and potatoes, and had no eye for fashion.

Ada was born in 1935 in Friuli, the Italian region north-west of Venice that is tucked between the Austrian Alps, Slovenia, and the northern reaches of the Adriatic Sea. She and her elder sister, Alfea (a third sister, Amelia, was later born in Canada) were raised on a farm in a desperately poor village just west of Udine, the Friuli capital, where the only potable water came from a single well in the main square. About a decade before the Second World War, her father, Benigno, went to Canada to make his fortune.

Ben, as he was known in Canada, was a tall, skinny redhead with a bulbous nose and John Lennon-style round eyeglasses. He was a veteran of Italy's victorious war against the remnants of the Austro-Hungarian empire, fought in 1918 when he was a teenager. He liked to fish and hunt and, like all peasant Italians of his era, was exceedingly careful with money. Handy with tools, he and his friends built their own homes. The idea of paying for contractors—"thieves!"—was completely alien to him. "He once spent $20 to fix the fridge and he never got over the feeling of being ripped off," my mother told me.

Ben had no formal education but taught himself to read and became a voracious consumer of non-fiction books. He claimed to have read the whole *Encyclopedia Britannica* over the years. (He never lost his heavy Italian accent. And though he was fluent in English, he had trouble pronouncing certain English words, like "Peanuts", which was the name of our pet dachshund when we were living in Chevy Chase, Maryland, in the late 1960s. Ben loved the low-slung little dog and would yell "Penis, come here Penis" as he wandered our dead-end street looking for her.)

Ben would return to Italy every few years during the 1930s, impregnate his wife, Regina, and leave. Regina was an illiterate, god-fearing peasant who was no more than five feet tall and shaped like a bowling pin. She had a heart of gold, was a fabulous cook, and knitted and prayed whenever she wasn't toiling in the kitchen and in the farm fields. I still have a drawer of thick wool socks that she made for me. She married Ben in 1931 in Friuli, lost a brother on the Eastern Front in the Second World War (his body was never found), and died at the age of ninety-nine in 2003 in Sudbury, a small city in northern Ontario with vast mining and smelting operations that were a magnet for immigrants.

When the Second World War broke out, Ben was working at the Inco mining company in Sudbury and could not make it back to Italy to rescue his family. Either that, or he was terrified to return home. He was still young enough to get press-ganged into Benito Mussolini's fascist army and sent to his slaughter in Albania, the Mediterranean, or North Africa. So, Regina packed up her two little girls, took a train to Genoa on the opposite coast of Italy, and boarded the *Conte di Savoia*, the Italian ocean liner famous for its high speed, to New York. My mother was four at the time and remembers the trip. The three of them had a cabin to themselves but the bunk mattresses were full of bedbugs. Alfea, my mother's older sister, then eight, was so traumatized by the bugs that she slept sitting in the cabin chair. The Italian government had given them a few silver coins to buy food aboard the ship. Alfea was sent to the commissary where she asked for "cioccolato" (chocolate). The commissary man, not following her northeastern Italian accent, gave her Chiclets instead. My grandmother and her daughters, who had no idea that Chiclets were for chewing, not eating, downed the whole pack and wondered why anyone would pay money for such tasteless candies.

They landed as refugees at the migrant centre at Ellis Island in April 1940, a year and a half before the Americans went to war against Germany and Italy. They crossed the border into Canada, joined Ben in Sudbury, and created a new life. Mom, like my father, had a joyless childhood. Her parents did not think education should be wasted on girls (few Italian girls made it beyond grade school in those years). Horrified at the prospect of a life as a domestic slave and baby mill, she fled to Toronto when she was in her mid-teens and worked as a switchboard operator for the Bell Telephone Company while finishing high school. She, like Dad, chose to rebel against the stifling cultural norms of immigrant families that would have handed her a bland and predictable life in small-town Canada.

She remembers being both charmed and repelled on meeting Bob Reguly in Toronto in November 1953, shortly after he finished his university degree. "He was wearing sailor-style bell-bottoms that were way out of fashion and his hair was plastered to his head," she told me. "His left eye had a white film over it and he looked terrible. But he was so funny. The first thing I said to him was, 'Can you see?' He said 'Of course not. I'm on a blind date.' That made me laugh."

Bob and Ada, and another couple on the date, went to a swanky downtown hotel for dinner and dancing. It was Grey Cup football weekend and the town was in party mode. The hotel wouldn't let my father into the dining room because he didn't have a tie. Always enterprising, like all good journalists, he told Ada to wait, rushed out and bought one at a nearby men's store. My mother says he was a lousy dancer but she was captivated by his wit and intelligence. They didn't see much of each other for a while, but Bob kept writing to her as he was pursuing his journalism career and they considered each other boyfriend and girlfriend.

His first reporting stint was at the *Winnipeg Free Press*. He hated his bosses and the city and lasted only a few months. He surfaced again at the *Timmins Daily Press*, a small newspaper in northeastern Ontario that was the first publication owned by press tycoon Roy Thomson, later Baron Thomson of Fleet. Two of the men he worked with, Peter Gzowski and Ted Byfield, would become famous journalists in their own right, and it was Byfield who would give me my first job in journalism, in late 1982, at the now-defunct *Alberta Report* weekly newsmagazine. Dad loved his days at Timmins, where zero-budget journalism demanded resourcefulness. Out-of-town work required him to jump on the newspaper delivery truck and time his interviews to the minute so he did not miss the truck on the rebound. He told me his assignment editor would give him precisely two disposable flash bulbs for his camera; that was how the then miserly Thomsons ran their newsrooms.

While she was working at Bell, Ada would sometimes visit Timmins by bus, several hours each way on the weekends. She and Bob were married in Sudbury in 1956, by which time Dad was working for another Thomson paper, the *Sudbury Star*. My mother remembers Dad's mother crying at the wedding, and not tears of joy. "She was upset because it was an Italian man who had arranged the abortion that killed her daughter and she was crying because I was Italian," my mother told me. "But she grew to love me. She was short and pudgy and very warm, and she hugged me hard all the time."

Dad evidently displayed early talent and was snatched up shortly after their European honeymoon in 1957 by the *Vancouver Province*, a true metropolitan newspaper and a big step up for a young reporter. I was born in Vancouver within a year of their arrival and we lived in a low-rise apartment building in English Bay, a funky part of town next to the beach and Stanley Park. A black and white photo in my mother's collection shows Dad and me playing in a pile of leaves in the park. It is one of the few photos of us together when I was young. He was an absentee father even back then, before his foreign adventures.[3]

Dad loved to compete, and his methods could be nasty. Once, covering a big court case, he unscrewed the mouthpieces of all the nearby pay phones and removed the transmitters, preventing rivals from calling in their copy to the news desks. When his paper merged with the *Vancouver Sun*, undermining the city's competitive newspaper dynamic, it was time for him to seek bigger adventures. Once again, he uprooted his wife, then a new mother, and joined the *Toronto Star* in 1958. My mother told me that their moves were hell on her. She was expected to do all the packing and take care of me, and later my sisters, Susan and Rebecca, while he was off boozing with the boys and banging away at his typewriter on late-night deadlines.

The *Star* was Ernest Hemingway's old paper, the largest and most glamorous rag in Canada. It was engaged in mortal combat with the *Toronto Telegram* and *The Globe and Mail*,[4] and as the premier show in town, it turned Bob Reguly into the hottest hack in the business.

---

3   In the early 2000s, when I was in Vancouver on a reporting assignment, I found the spot where we lived. It was surrounded by high-rise condo buildings. I can't imagine how it has survived the city's development onslaught.

4   *The Globe and Mail* is the paper I would join in 1997 after long stints working in New York with the *Financial Post* (now *National Post*), and in London with *The Times*.

CHAPTER 3

The Razzle-Dazzle Reporter

ORONTO AND OTTAWA, *via Alaska and Brooklyn, 1958–1964*—
Journalism, of course, is not what it once was. Every reporter of a
certain age knows that, and every reader. Before the Internet and
Twitter, before smartphones and laptop computers, before twenty-four-
hour TV news and shock radio jocks and stories that are massaged to death
by armies of PR men and women, it was newspapers that set the agenda.
Newsrooms were a man's world (women reporters and editors, like Hildy
Johnson in the 1940 film *His Girl Friday*, were a rarity), competition was ferocious, and smoking, hard drinking, and fighting were *de rigueur*. The ability
to produce scoops, and lots of them, would make or break a reporter's career.

My father was a walking caricature of a newsman of his era. One of my
favourite photographs shows him at his typewriter, cigarette dangling from
his lips, a cocky grin lighting up his face. Dad was the sort of reporter for
whom the word "intrepid" might have been invented, as former *Globe and
Mail* writer Michael Posner said in his full-page obituary. Armed with a pen,
notepad, smokes, and a pocket full of change for payphones, Dad handed
the *Toronto Star* some of its biggest exclusive stories in its history, since it
began in 1892.

Investigative journalism was not born in the 1960s but it flourished in that decade and in the 1970s. The *Pentagon Papers*, Watergate, and the thalidomide scandal were three of the biggest investigative stories. Back then, newspapers had fat budgets, a deep sense of social responsibility, and ferocious competitive instincts. They could afford to send their reporters on lengthy, truth-seeking missions that risked producing nothing of value. I know that my father, in the prime of his career and even in his twilight years, when he was yearning to recapture some of his former glory, spent enormous amounts of time chasing sensational stories that he believed to be true but could never prove. One was about a secret Canadian helicopter team in Vietnam that was wiped out by Viet Cong guerrillas; another about a hidden Cuban terrorist training camp in the wilderness of Quebec; still another about his belief that an Avro Canada CF-105 Arrow interceptor jet was secretly flown to the United States in 1959, minutes after Prime Minister John Diefenbaker killed off the costly, world-leading aerospace project. Many stories never came to fruition. But when his reporting hit the mark, it hit big.

My mother told me that my father started as a low-level desk editor at the *Star* before jumping into the reporting shark tank. Desk editors handled reporters' stories, eliminating superfluous words or paragraphs, fixing grammar and spelling, and insisting on rewrites or extra reporting if the story that landed on their desks was sloppy. The first byline I could find in the *Star* archives appeared on April 27, 1959, deservedly buried on page twelve of the front section, next to ads for twenty-one-inch Admiral round-tube TVs for $189, six-piece Swedish dinettes for $119 and Arborite-top desks for $19.95. His story, datelined Sudbury, was about the Ontario provincial Liberal leader calling for the Conservative government to set up a department to spur development in the "neglected north." As dull as it was, there was not a wasted word in the piece.

His career prospects would soon improve. In the early 1960s, he was sent to Ottawa, where he joined the parliamentary press gallery. I remember nothing of that era other than my father's beaten-up green Ford family sedan, a Fairlane. He loved cars, although he could never afford anything swish and, remarkably, never had an accident even though he had only one working eye.

From Ottawa, he graduated to one of his early adventures, covering the Alaska earthquake of March 27, 1964 that, at 9.2, remains the biggest earthquake ever recorded in North America and the second most powerful in the world. One of the first reporters to arrive in Anchorage, he wrote a piece about the lucky escapes of some of the survivors, including "the housewife who was in her kitchen when the rest of the house slid down a bluff into the water. She climbed to the kitchen roof and was rescued by a helicopter."

His first big break, and the story that propelled him into Canadian journalism's big leagues, was Hal Banks.

Harold Chamberlain Banks was an Iowa-born American thug, a burly, arrogant, sarcastic control freak who sported knife-fight scars on his right hand and a bullet scar on his right hip. He arrived in Canada in the spring of 1949, at the age of forty, to break the allegedly communist Canadian Seamen's Union (CSU), whose many strikes, most of them illegal, had closed Canada's ports. He had been invited by Canadian shipowners enraged at the CSU's effectiveness. They had appealed for help to the rival Seafarers International Union of the United States, which had a small presence in Canada. The objective was to rid the Canadian waterfront of the CSU and replace it with the Seafarers' International Union of Canada (SIU) under Banks, a former deckhand who had been an SIU organizer in California and who had done three years in San Quentin State Prison for bouncing cheques after his acquittal on charges of murder, burglary, carrying dangerous weapons, and child abduction.

The shipowners were mostly wealthy Montreal men with extensive political connections to the government of the day, so Banks's presence in Canada was supported by Prime Minister Louis St. Laurent's Liberals, who conveniently ignored all his criminal charges and convictions and gave him landed immigrant status. Banks smashed the CSU and absorbed many of its members into the SIU, making him the undisputed czar of Canada's 15,000 merchant-marine sailors. His methods were brutal: his goon squads used axe handles, chains, and sawed-off shotguns to break through CSU pickets during a 1949 strike so that SIU scabs could take over the ships. Many CSU members were injured; a few died.

Banks was soon billed as Canada's answer to Jimmy Hoffa, the notorious US Teamsters union leader who would later disappear, the probable victim of a Mafia hit. Like Hoffa, he had his supporters. He made the ships run on time. He was credited with breaking the "Stalin-dominated CSU," even though there was zero evidence that the union had any Soviet connections. His devotees referred to him as "Prince Hal". But his infamous "Do Not Ship" list meant that anyone he considered a communist lost his job. In practice, most of the 4,000 names on the list were men who simply disagreed with him or disobeyed his orders. He used looted SIU money to finance a lavish lifestyle in Montreal, which included a white Cadillac that was traded in for a new one every year, and a wardrobe of 300 expensive suits. He continued to enjoy direct access to the Liberal government's inner circles, which secretly and disgracefully supported his thuggish behaviour.

Peter Gzowski, my father's old colleague and roommate from his Timmins days, would describe Banks in a *Maclean's* magazine cover story as "a violent labour despot whose abuses of men and funds are on the record but whose grip on power has survived every effort to break it." But in time, Banks's violent, criminal life became too blatant to be ignored. In the 1950s, as his power expanded, he was charged with assault, possession of a sawed-off shotgun, smuggling cigarettes, and libel. He beat them all, except for the minor smuggling charge. Justice Thomas G. Norris's blistering report said, "Banks is the stuff of the Capones and the Hoffas, of whom the dictators throughout history, from the earliest times to the totalitarians, Hitler and Stalin, are prototypes."

Banks slipped out of Canada in 1962, a wanted man. The RCMP and the FBI launched a manhunt, to no success. More than a few old members of the Liberal government were no doubt happy to see him go. The *Star* handed Dad the Banks file in 1964 and the results were spectacular. On October 1, the *Star* front page blared: "Star Man finds Hal Banks."

Dad found Banks within two hours of reaching New York, although he must have been tipped off, by whom, I do not know. I do know that by that time he had superb political, police, and intelligence contacts. He also had street smarts and probably figured that Banks would retreat to familiar territory, where he could surround himself with bully-boy allies. Dad hired a taxi and toured the known SIU properties. Next to a wharf near Flatbush, Brooklyn, he spotted a white Cadillac with Quebec licence plates parked next to a yacht. A portly man was reclining on the dock beside the yacht.

"Hal Banks?" my father asked.

"Yeah, waddya want?" Banks replied.

Dad told him he was a *Toronto Star* reporter and wanted an interview. Banks said, "I don't want to speak to you. Beat it!"

My father promptly obliged, retreating to a local camera store, where he bought a US$10 Kodak Brownie camera and a roll of film. He returned to the wharf within the hour, well aware that Banks, prone to casual violence, did not want to be found and surrounded himself with hooligans. Did Dad know he was risking his life by going back to Banks's yacht? Probably. But he was onto a scoop and wasn't going to let go.

Dad snapped away, capturing images of Banks until the man's goons gave chase. One of them bashed Dad on the back of his head with a black-jack, opening his scalp.

Here is what my father wrote in the piece that launched his career as Canada's hotshot reporter. He was thirty-three years old.

> I found Hal Banks yesterday—sitting all alone on a union yacht docked in Mill Basin here, the familiar cigarette clenched in his teeth. . . . At my approach Banks ducked into the boat and several guards charged at me . . . One of them managed to hit me on the head . . . I ran down six-lane Flatbush Ave., dodging traffic with four goons in hot pursuit. But luckily the driver of the car I had rented—a man who knew his way around the waterfront—had wheeled around and came roaring at my pursuers. He nudged them out of the way with some fancy steering. I hopped in and we sped off, pursued by a white Chevrolet which we soon shook off.

The story was a sensation and John Diefenbaker, then leader of the Conservative opposition in parliament, paid my father the ultimate compliment by suggesting the RCMP hire Reguly. "What the government with all its resources was unable to achieve has now been accomplished by the press," he said.

In addition to embarrassing the FBI, the RCMP, and Canada's Liberal government—Diefenbaker called Banks "the pampered pet of

Liberalism"—Dad's scoop got Banks arrested. He was refused bail and flung into the clink in Brooklyn. Canada filed an extradition request for Banks to face a perjury charge linked to a conspiracy charge, but the US refused it on the grounds that conspiracy was not an extraditable offence. Banks was released from custody. The old Liberals who had covertly supported him were no doubt relieved that he would not face a trial in Canada that would see him hang the party's dirty laundry from the courtroom rafters. Banks moved to San Francisco, where he had originally worked for the SIU, and died there in 1985 at the age of seventy-six.

I was too young to remember the Hal Banks scoop, but when I was a bit older I was thrilled to learn the story of the goons chasing my father through traffic while his scalp oozed blood. "Did you really get bashed on the head?" I asked, wondering if he had added a little Hollywood drama to the saga. He insisted that he had and parted his thick dark hair with his fingers to reveal a white scar on the back of his head. He told me the gash required stiches. I felt the scar; it was real and my admiration for my father soared.

Decades later, I am still in awe of his exploits. Would I have gone after Banks, knowing he was surrounded by armed thugs? I don't know. I do know that my instinct is to run away from burning houses, not towards them. Dad was the opposite. My mother says her husband certainly was brave. But she is also convinced that his brain's neurocircuitry simply did not register fear like ordinary humans. This was a man who parachuted into forest fires with alacrity, who took crazy risks in covering wars, and was kidnapped in the Middle East and calmly faced down his would-be executioner. How much was courage, and how much a glitch in his fight-or-flight response? I will never know.

Despite the importance of the Hal Banks story, the best was yet to come for my father. Two years later, in 1966, he landed the biggest scoop in the history of Canadian newspapers.

CHAPTER 4

The Sex-Spy Scandal

MUNICH, GERMANY, 1966—As I pressed the buzzer on the door of the apartment block on a busy central Munich street, I wondered how my dad felt when he stood in the same spot forty-five years earlier. I did not know who would answer the door. He did. It would be a glamorous East German prostitute and Soviet agent named Gerda Munsinger. It was 1966 and the height of the Cold War and everyone thought she was dead. Only my father and the editor of the *Toronto Star* suspected a cover-up and had the gumption to pursue the story. It was at this apartment that Dad found Munsinger very much alive.

The "Munsinger Affair," as it was known, read like a Cold War thriller. It was Canada's first genuine sex-spy scandal, a home-grown variant of Britain's sensational Profumo Affair of the same era. The elements were similar: a senior Cabinet minister having an affair with a glamorous woman whose pillow talk may have been channelled back to the Soviets. At the time, in the late 1950s and early 1960s, Canada was a major force within NATO and a front-line ally with the Americans, the British, and the West Germans in the effort to root out Soviet spies and agents from their midst. The geopolitics of the era were tense: the Cold War threatened to turn hot at any time, as it almost did in 1962 in the Cuban Missile Crisis, a nuclear standoff between the United States and the USSR.

The Munsinger scandal began on March 4, 1966. John Diefenbaker, opposition leader (and Conservative prime minister between 1957 and 1963), was berating Justice Minister Lucien Cardin in the House of Commons over a security matter involving a postal clerk who allegedly had been working with the Soviets at some junior level. Cardin blew his top, insisting that Diefenbaker was the very last person to give the government advice on security measures. "I want the Right Honourable member to tell the House about the participation of the Monsignor case when he was prime minister," he blurted out, mangling Munsinger's name.

The Ottawa press gallery went into a frenzy. For years, reporters had been hearing rumours of an RCMP investigation into a mysterious woman from East Germany and her connection to certain cabinet ministers in Diefenbaker's government. The next day, the *Star*'s Martin Goodman, a big name in the newsroom, reported that the RCMP had a photograph of "Monsignor" in a compromising position with an unnamed former senior member of the government.

But was the woman alive? It had been reported in the press, and said in the House of Commons some time earlier, that she had died of leukemia in 1964, two years after leaving Canada. Since she was believed to be dead, the Ottawa press gallery's initial spasm of interest soon fizzled. A day after Cardin's outburst in the House of Commons, Lester Pearson, the Liberal prime minister and Diefenbaker's successor, appointed an Ontario judge to head an inquiry into "Monsignor." The press moved on to other stories.

The *Star*'s editors were not convinced she was dead. On March 5, Dad was put on the case. He was the logical choice, having proved his investigative worth with Hal Banks. He had become the go-to reporter when editors wanted quick results on a big story. By then, he was also well connected, having worked with police and intelligence services, and having served on the parliamentary beat in Ottawa.

Gerda Munsinger, as Dad pieced together her astonishing life, had been born Gerda Heseler in the city of Königsberg, East Prussia (now Kaliningrad, Russia) in 1929. Her politics were inherited from her father, who was labelled a communist sympathizer by the Nazis in 1943 and shot in Dresden. She claimed she landed in a Soviet concentration camp after the Second World War and was a prisoner until 1948. Another story says she was living with a major in Soviet intelligence in East Berlin in the years immediately after the war, and that she crossed the border between East and West Germany several times and was arrested for espionage by the American border police in 1949. The *Encyclopedia of Cold War Espionage, Spies, and Secret Operations* says that Western intelligence officers picked up "some information" that Gerda had spied for the Russians in the late 1940s, worked as a prostitute and engaged in petty crime, and had lived with a Soviet intelligence officer.

She later surfaced in Hamburg as a housemaid to a senior officer in the British Army on the Rhine and landed a job as a waitress in the private dining room at SHAPE, Supreme Headquarters Allied Powers Europe, where she served lunches to Supreme Allied Commander Dwight Eisenhower, who was SHAPE commander in 1951 and 1952 before becoming President of the United States in 1953. She also provided secretarial services to Eisenhower and his wife, Mamie. After Eisenhower left Europe, she moved to Garmisch-Partenkirchen in Bavaria, the site of a US Army spy school, where she had an affair with a US general and married Michael Munsinger, a military policeman and demobilized soldier from Brooklyn. The marriage soured after she was blocked from returning to the United States with him, but she used her new surname to enter Canada in 1955. Three years earlier, when she was Gerda Heseler, she had attempted to get into Canada but was refused entry for security reasons.

Munsinger settled in Montreal. Tall, blonde and exotic—my father, never politically correct, spoke of her "gawk-worthy superstructure"—she quickly gained a party-girl reputation, joining a stable of call girls run by Willie Obront. Obront was a gangster, loan shark, money launderer, and the Canadian associate of the notorious American mobster Meyer Lansky. Munsinger soon became a star attraction at Conservative Party events, where she caught the leering attention of several cabinet ministers. One of them was George Hees, nicknamed "Gorgeous George", a bon vivant who was regarded as the second most powerful man in the Tory party. Munsinger once spent the night with him at the posh Château Laurier hotel in Ottawa.

Unimpressed by his performance, she later told him, "As a lover, you make a great politician."

When the Munsinger scandal broke, Hees lambasted my father for ruining his inevitable rise to the office of prime minister. I am sure Dad took it as a compliment and would never have apologized—not his style. Hees ran for leadership of the Conservative Party in 1967, a year after the Munsinger case exploded, and got nowhere, although he remained in parliament until 1988, eight years before his death.

Munsinger's more enduring affair was with associate defence minister Pierre Sévigny, a politician admired by the press gallery scribblers for his Gallic bonhomie and approachable style. His affair with the beautiful German lasted three years and caught the attention of the RCMP. Sévigny was a Second World War hero and had lost a leg in the Battle of the Rhineland in 1945. He paid the rent on Munsinger's downtown Montreal apartment. The RCMP believed Russians were listening to Sévigny's pillow talk with Munsinger. The RCMP spy catchers bugged Munsinger's bedroom and played a tape of a tryst to Prime Minister Diefenbaker, who was startled by a thud at the start of their love-making. It was the sound of Sévigny's artificial leg hitting the floor after he hopped into bed.

Diefenbaker asked Sévigny to explain his relationship with the woman. Sévigny replied that if members of parliament were expelled for having affairs, the prime minister would not have a government. Incredibly, Diefenbaker allowed Sévigny to remain in cabinet, where he survived until the government was defeated in the election of 1963. By then, Munsinger was long gone and reported dead in government files. When and how this misinformation landed in the files is not known. Her "death" was tactically brilliant; it quashed the investigation into her rumoured role as a Soviet honeytrap agent. Until my father came along.

In fact, it was Obront who had whisked her away, my father later learned. Obront's chauffeur drove her all the way to Sydney, Nova Scotia, a 1,500-kilometre slog, to catch a flight to Gander, Newfoundland and then on to West Germany. The route cleverly covered up the trail.

Dad knew Obront and even told me he liked him. I don't know how they met but it seems natural that they would find each other's orbits. My father was an investigative reporter and would have been well aware from his police contacts of Obront's underworld activities in Montreal. Moreover, Obront was not in hiding. He claimed he was a legitimate businessman running his family meat-packing company. Over the years, the two would spar with one another, trading lies, truths and half-truths as each hunted for clues as to what the other knew.[5]

In a note written to me three decades after the fact, Dad told me how Obront handed him the tip that would crack the Munsinger case wide:

> When the Munsinger affair rose in parliament, I immediately tapped him. He admitted he had known Gerda, lied that she had been an elevator operator at Eaton's store [a department store chain with outlets in Montreal]. When was that? He gave dates. They were long after she had reportedly died. So Obront unwittingly revealed that she was still alive and the hunt was on.

But where was she? My father did not know. No one even knew her real name, which had been variously reported as "Olga Monsignor" and "Olga Munzinger". Dad's first job was to verify her name so he could track her down. He did it the old-fashioned way—he outranked a contact.

His victim was a former member of Diefenbaker's staff. Dad took him to the Montreal Press Club and ordered drinks with abandon. Here is what he told Canadian journalist Scott Alexander, whose piece on the Munsinger affair, "Read all about it: *Star* man finds Gerda Munsinger," appeared in *Content* magazine in 1976, and was later reprinted in a book, *The News: Inside the Canadian Media* (1982):

---

5 In 1973, after my father left the *Star* and joined CTV's weekly investigative programme, *W5*, he managed to interview Obront—the only on-camera interview Obront ever did—and peppered him with questions about his alleged tax evasion. Obront later tried to buy off my father, after realizing that his on-air questions could put him under investigation. "I scoffed that he couldn't reach me through bribes or beating," my father told me. "Obront said, 'How would you like your son run over by a truck?'" Evidently, Dad did not take the threat seriously enough to mention to my mother or me. Obront was arrested in Florida in 1983 for trafficking cocaine, was sentenced to twenty years in prison, and died in 2017.

> At 2 a.m., I ran out of money and phoned the night desk to please wire
> $200 fast. I told them I was in a drinking contest and the night edi-
> tor said, "It sounds like you've already lost" . . . The government aide
> fenced for a couple of hours, but in the end, he just had too much to
> drink. I was slapping him with doubles for four solid hours. When he
> gave me the correct name as Gerda Munsinger and confirmed she had
> been connected with Sévigny, I was so far gone I wasn't even sure I'd
> heard correctly. The strange thing is, he told me in front of dozens of
> other reporters and not one of them picked it up.

Obront's sloppy lie confirmed that the mystery woman was alive. The
drunken government aide had confirmed that her name was "Gerda
Munsinger." Finding where she was living was the missing piece. Dad went
to see another of his contacts, an Israeli spook in Montreal. This spy had
good German connections and called East German security headquarters in
East Berlin, routing the call through Helsinki and Warsaw to disguise that it
had been placed from Montreal. They confirmed the woman was alive and
living in West Germany. Dad was given no other information.

By then, my father and his editors, terrified that the competition was
on the case, went into overdrive. Dad found Munsinger's old Montreal
address from a 1960 phone directory. He asked Robert McKenzie, one of
the *Star*'s journalists in Quebec, to check out the building, on Rue Front.
McKenzie learned that the building's janitor and his wife were friends of
Munsinger, and that she had sent them a letter in 1965 from her friend's
house in Mondsee, Austria, which she also used as the return address.
A German-speaking photographer at the *Star* called the Mondsee family,
who told him that Munsinger had been working at the Operon Café in
Munich.

That was on Wednesday, March 9, 1966. Dad packed his bag. But before
heading to the airport, he called Sévigny, who vigorously denied knowing
Munsinger or ever having heard of her. Hours later, Dad was on a flight to
Munich via London. A CBC TV reporter, Norman DePoe, was on the same
flight, to cover the British election. Sitting uncomfortably next to DePoe,
my father explained that he was also covering the election and agreed to

meet him for dinner in London, before slipping away at Heathrow Airport and boarding the next flight to Munich. He went straight to the Operon Café and talked to the manager, who was not revealing anything. Dad lost his patience and smacked him a few times. "I just didn't have time to play games with the guy," he told *Content* magazine. "I guess he was frightened. He gave me her address."

This was not as unusual occurrence. In that era, reporters were known to rough up sources if they needed information, or so my father told me. He added that his newsroom colleagues would even get into drunken brawls with their editors, and that fights with the bosses outside the newsroom would not get you fired.

Now armed with the address, Dad went to 1 Ainmillerstrasse and found "G. Munsinger" next to apartment No. 5 in the lobby. He banged on the door. There was no answer. He staked out the building, waiting for a tall blonde to enter. One did and the light went on in apartment No. 5. He banged on the door again. When Munsinger opened the door, my father introduced himself. The woman's eyes widened. "Perhaps it's about Sévigny?" she asked, and started babbling.

She later explained to my father that she was in a panic: "I thought you had been sent by Willie Obront to kill me," she told him. As they were talking, the phone rang and Dad heard Munsinger say, "It's too late, he's already here."

It was Sévigny. An hour later, Dad had arranged for a freelance photographer to visit Munsinger's apartment. In a fine example of chequebook journalism, Ralph Allen, the *Star*'s fearless and beloved editor and a former war correspondent, demanded exclusive access to Munsinger and wired C$1,000 to my father with which to lock her down as a *Star* source. Dad drew up a contract on a piece of scrap paper and handed her the money. The payment worked. The Munsinger story would be Allen's last great coup as editor. He died nine months after the story was published at age fifty-three. My father said that he was the greatest editor he had ever worked for.

Dad phoned in the story from the home of the *Star*'s Munich stringer. To put the competition off the scent, Allen had the *Star*'s presses run off several thousand first-edition copies with no mention of Munsinger. Those

copies were picked up by the couriers from the rival Toronto papers. The
ruse worked. The night editors of the *The Toronto Telegram* and *The Globe
and Mail* read the front pages of the *Star* and breathed easily, relieved not
to have been scooped on the Munsinger affair.

Allen then let loose with all barrels blazing in the second edition. The
144-point typeface headline was the size normally reserved for the end of
world wars. "STAR MAN FINDS GERDA MUNSINGER", it blared.
Here are the opening paragraphs:

> MUNICH—The girl Canada calls Olga Munsinger is alive and well.
>
> Her real name is Gerda Munsinger. She is tall, blonde and shapely.
>
> I found her in a chintzy flat in an affluent district of Munich, wearing a
> gold September birthstone ring that was the gift of a former Canadian
> cabinet minister.

Over at the *Telegram*, the editors were feeling pretty good about themselves; they had managed to find old photos of Munsinger and ran them
in the first edition. While they were boozing after their late-evening work
shift, the *Star*'s second edition landed like a bunker-buster bomb. "We were
simply outclassed," Andrew MacFarlane, the *Telegram*'s managing editor
at the time, later told *Content* magazine. "It was the worst thing that ever
happened to me . . . I still have nightmares about it."

The next few days were a blur for my father and Ray Timson, the *Star*
reporter, and later managing editor, who was sent to Munich to help sew
up the story. My father noticed he was being tailed wherever he went and
assumed his follower was West German intelligence. Journalists from across
Canada and Europe were jammed into the lobby of Munsinger's building.
A pair of window washers lowered themselves to her front window. Dad
had a hunch that they were photographers in disguise and snapped the
curtains shut just as they whipped out their cameras. Convinced that his
phone at the Bayerischer Hof hotel was tapped, he paid off the switchboard girls to divert calls to another phone. A *Telegram* reporter slipped
a note under Munsinger's door, offering her US$10,000 for five minutes

of her time. The German media offered her US$50,000 for her story and picture rights. The *Star*, for a fee, gave the CBC the rights to a one-shot TV interview and DePoe, the reporter who Dad had deceived on their London flight, was diverted to Munich. To get Munsinger safely to the studio, my father, Timson, and the CBC found a woman who looked like Munsinger, dressed her up in an overcoat and shawl and pushed her though the mob of reporters outside to a waiting car while the real Munsinger slipped out of the building and into a red sports car. The *Telegram*'s man, Don Grant, hailed a cab to chase the fake Munsinger. As they were speeding down the street in hot pursuit, the cab fishtailed on some ice and crashed.

The story electrified Canadians for weeks. Munsinger admitted having affairs with a number of Conservative cabinet ministers, including Sévigny, but denied she was engaged in espionage. The *Star* handed Dad and Timson C$2,500 in play money, a small fortune back then, as a reward for a job well done. The duo stopped in London on their way home and partied hard for five days. "We spent money like it was going out of style," Dad told *Content* magazine.

In the end, the "Report of the Commission of Inquiry into the Affairs of One Gerda Munsinger", published half a year after Dad found her in Munich, did not conclude she was a Soviet agent (although Dad believed she was). It did say that she had posed a security risk and it determined that Diefenbaker should have removed Sévigny from his cabinet post when he learned about the affair in 1960. A friend of mine, a former Montreal TV journalist who knew Sévigny, said the politician had called Munsinger "the best piece of ass I ever had," and was seething mad at my father for having exposed their long fling. Charles Lynch, who was Ottawa bureau chief for the old Southam newspaper chain at the time, thought the Munsinger scandal helped Canada sex up its "dull and unexciting image," and encouraged more tourists to visit Montreal's Expo 67. It may have.

While the Munsinger affair didn't put anyone on trial for espionage, it did make "Robert Reguly" a household name and guaranteed the *Star*'s reputation as Canada's premier razzle-dazzle paper and scoop machine. Growing up knowing that Dad had unearthed a scandal that shook the political world of Canada and was as important an event as the Profumo Affair in Britain, filled me with awe and pride.

In 2011, only a few months after my father died, my youngest daughter, Emma, then aged eleven, and her schoolmates won a spot on a German TV game show. The program was to be taped in Munich before a live audience, so Emma, her sister Arianna, then aged fourteen, and my wife, Karen Zagor, jumped on a plane. As luck would have it, our hotel was walking distance to 1 Ainmillerstrasse.

I had hoped the apartment building would fulfil my Cold War fantasies. I imagined a dark, foreboding building that could have served as a backdrop for an Orson Welles film or John le Carré story. Sadly, it was anything but. Five storeys high, it had obviously been remodelled. The exterior was clad in what looked like beige plaster and the apartment window frames were made of aluminum. An optician and a hairdresser were among the building's street-level shops. I pressed the buzzer. I do not speak German and had no idea how I would explain my desire to see the apartment. There was no answer. I made a second attempt an hour later. Again, no answer. I gave up and went back to our hotel.

Over the decades, I must have talked to my father dozens of times about Munsinger over dinner or on the porch of our cottage, but I never took notes. We were just talking as father and son. Later, curious as a journalist as to how the old Reguly scoop machine worked, I pored over the published Munsinger reports and came to realize that he revealed details to me that he probably had told no one else. One of them was the name of the Israeli intelligence agent in Montreal who confirmed to my father that Munsinger was alive and living in West Germany, the tip he needed before heading there. I remember the man's name and jotted it in my diary about fifteen years ago, but Dad made me promise never to reveal it, although I can say that his first name was Peter. My efforts to find Peter failed and I don't know if the full name Dad gave me was his real name or a false name used as a cover.

A year or two after my father's death, I was rummaging through filing cabinets in the basement of my parents' house in Toronto. I was looking for anything—photos, notes, newspaper clippings—that would help reconstruct my father's life. My idea back then was simply to write a few thousand words about his remarkable career for my two daughters. In a dark corner, I noticed a framed picture about half the size of a regular TV screen. I picked it up. The glass was broken and the picture was a bit mouldy. It was a chalk portrait of Munsinger that she had sent to my father in the 1970s. I do not remember having seen it myself before my father died.

At the bottom of the portrait, which made her look her glamorous best, she had written in English "To Bob, with my warmest wishes, Gerda." Reading those few words, I wondered if she had a soft spot for my father. Maybe she had a crush on him, or maybe she was simply grateful that he made her famous for a brief shining moment. I will never know. She died in relative obscurity in 1998 in Munich, at age sixty-nine, by which time she had married for a third time and was known as Gerda Merkt. The biography she claimed to be writing, *To Whom It May Concern*, was never published.

The Munsinger story won my father a National Newspaper Award. In the summer of 1966, just a few months after Dad's Munich escapade, the *Star* rewarded him the Washington, DC bureau.

CHAPTER 5

Prelude to a War

CHEVY CHASE, SUMMER, 1966—The Reguly family rolled into Chevy Chase, Maryland, in a banged-up 1961 red Volkswagen Beetle with three little kids—my younger sisters, Susan and Rebecca, and me—and a fat brown dachshund named Peanuts all stuffed in the back seat. It was high summer, no air conditioning, and the heat and humidity were punishing for a Canadian family used to cooler climes.

My mother and father smoked during the entire trip from Toronto, about 750 kilometres. They were excited, but nervous. They were young—Dad was thirty-five, Mum thirty-one—and were about to enter a strange new world. Chevy Chase, on the border of Washington, DC, was one of the wealthiest, most powerful neighbourhoods in the world, and still is. They must have felt like bumpkins as they parked in front of 6917 Woodside Place, the big, sandy brown, wood-sided house they had rented for US$300 a month, a fortune back then for a reporter. It had a lush, expansive garden and was one of only nine houses on the street, each of them equipped with perfectly manicured lawns and driveways filled with expensive cars. Toronto it was not.

Chevy Chase had a population of about 10,000 and was officially a town but, in reality, was a staid old bedroom community for Washington's power brokers. It was full of congressmen, lawyers, journalists, lobbyists, doctors, retired military officers, senior government officials and, no doubt, intelligence officers, all of them white. Until the late 1940s, it was, infamously, a "Sundown town," meaning that it used local exclusion laws to keep non-whites from buying or renting property. The term comes from signs that said that "coloured people" had to make themselves scarce by "sundown." By the time we moved there, those laws were long gone but the only African-Americans I remember seeing were gardeners, garbage collectors, and cleaning ladies.

My sister Susan and I were sent to Chevy Chase Elementary School, just down the street, a fixture in the neighbourhood since 1917. As Canadians, it struck as strange to have to start each day placing our right hands over our hearts and pledging allegiance to the American flag. Every two weeks or so, the school would test the big yellow air-raid sirens installed on the top of tall poles in the playground. When they blared, we would all scramble to the school basement, get on our hands and knees, and tuck ourselves under the wooden tables. The exercise was not scary. We were too young to understand that we could be obliterated by Soviet missiles; the term "Cold War" meant nothing to us. It was just routine that made us giggle.

Rebecca, my youngest sibling, was a baby and pretty much full-time work for my mother, who was frazzled from switching cities and holding the family together while her husband's career took off. Still, the neighbours on Woodside Place were gregarious and welcoming, and the traffic-free street meant the kids ran freely in packs, hopping from one backyard to another, running through lawn sprinklers, climbing trees, and snatching ice cream treats from bored, stay-at-home mothers. Doors were rarely locked and the milkman would place quarts of milk in glass jugs, and popsicles for the kids, directly into the fridge. The whole place had the feel of a swanky country club even though it was on the edge of a thriving capital city, one that was about to go into turmoil as the Vietnam War and civil rights movements heated up.

The rambling old house across the street was occupied by a Navy reserve officer and his wife, Gene and Rene Kelley, who had an open-yard policy. There was always a beer and a barbecue ready for whoever wanted to drop in. Owner of a real-estate business, Gene was tall and handsome, and the ladies on the street would swoon when he dressed up in his smart, white Navy uniform. Bikinis were just coming into fashion then. My mother bought one, walked over to the Kelleys' circular drive, and modelled it for Gene and Rene. Later, Rene said that Gene was "speechless" at the sight of the Italian beauty wearing almost nothing. Not long after, the other young mothers on the street ran out to buy bikinis.

The neighbours to the left were the Pearsons. James B. Pearson was the Republican senator from Kansas. He held moderate views and sometimes supported progressive Democratic legislation from President Lyndon B. Johnson, who was pushing through his Great Society reforms, aimed at eliminating poverty and racial injustice. When we moved to Chevy Chase, the US presence in Vietnam was still in its optimistic early stages and victory was assumed. LBJ had expanded the American presence greatly in 1965 when he committed the first American fighting battalions to South Vietnam and launched Operation Rolling Thunder, the name given to the sustained aerial bombing of communist North Vietnam.

Pearson was in favour of the Vietnam War, as were most congressmen and senators. They were confident that the mighty US military would score a quick victory and stop what they assumed was a grand nefarious plan, directed by Moscow and Beijing, to install client-state communist governments throughout Southeast Asia. Many Americans, including Pearson, would change their view as the war slogged on, American body bags piled up, and the streets filled with anti-war protestors. By early 1968, shortly after Joan Baez's powerful anti-war song *Saigon Bride* was climbing the charts, a Gallup poll showed that 50 per cent of Americans disapproved of LBJ's handling of the war.

As kids, we were oblivious to the war, at least until Dad went to Vietnam in 1967, the year after we moved to Chevy Chase. As a boy, I just wanted to have fun with my new friends. The senator's youngest daughter, Laura, who was a few years older than me, would be the first girl I ever kissed. I played spin-the-bottle with her and her friends in the Pearson family garden. I was probably nine and remember that kiss as if it were yesterday.

But it was the McGettigans, who lived to our right, who would come to dominate our lives and enrich it in every way. Valerie and Jim McGettigan were a few years older than my parents and had three children, Lizanne, Kim and Kevin, who about matched the ages of the three Reguly kids. Valerie was a gregarious, glamorous firecracker of Polish descent who immediately adopted my mother as the sister she never had and implemented a no-knock, open-door policy. In effect, the families merged. Even Peanuts became communal property. Valerie was an interior decorator who could play the piano well and could throw a boozy bash or an elegant dinner party with effortless charm and grace. Jim spent the late Second World War years in the US Coast Guard, trained as an architect and, like my father, never turned down a drink. He shared Dad's love of words. Both were master raconteurs and loved a good joke. Jim was especially fond of Middle English and could recite the *Canterbury Tales* or invent a Middle English-style poem in a second, depending on the lubricants coursing through his veins.

Kim McGettigan, who is still a beloved friend of mine, as are her siblings, remembers the Regulys penetrating their staid, tight-knit community like a grenade. She told me in 2020:

> As Canadians, there were seen as comfortably exotic. Bob was a gregarious demigod, Ada a dusky beauty. They were bold and fiery and sexy . . . No one could command a room like Bob Reguly. There was an underlying tension, though, as Jim [Kim's father] believed himself to be the alpha wolf until the Regulys appeared. Bob was catnip to the ladies of Chevy Chase, with careless good looks and an animal magnetism that proved heady. It did not go unnoticed by the men on the block . . . As devastated as Ada was when Bob got his assignment to cover the war in Vietnam, the men of Woodside Place collectively breathed a sigh of relief. They welcomed a respite from the apex predator among the sheep.

Dad soon bought a more socially acceptable car, a new Ford Falcon station wagon, in "frost turquoise," and joined the National Press Club, which was housed in the National Press Building near the White House. Built in 1927, the imposing fourteen-storey block was home to the thousands of domestic and foreign reporters who covered the White House and the American political and economic scene. The press club helped make life easy for its members. They could schmooze each other for contacts and chat up lobbyists and congressional staffers in the bar, where no photos were the rule and off-the-record conversations were assumed. Often, the news came gift-wrapped for them, as when the great and the good showed up at the club to deliver their messages and grab some headlines. Soviet premier Nikita Khrushchev, French president Charles de Gaulle, and Indian prime minister Indira Gandhi all made appearances in the 1950s and 1960s.

I remember visiting Dad's press club office a couple of times. It was a comfortable little mess with a tattered leather sofa and a big, black Underwood typewriter moored on the desk. In the evenings, when the reporters in the building were on deadline, the roar of typewriter keys hitting the rollers was glorious. Dad often wrote from his home office, too, and when he did, the Reguly children would fall asleep to the oddly comforting staccato rhythm of typing: long pauses followed by intense clatter as inspiration hit and his fingers pounded.

He had plenty to write about that first year in DC, from the war's impact on American lives and foreign relations to the rise of Martin Luther King, whose peaceful anti-war and anti-racism rallies in Washington, Chicago, and Selma, Alabama were rattling LBJ. At the time, the ties between LBJ and Lester B. Pearson, the Canadian prime minister who had won the Nobel Peace Prize for his role in resolving the 1956 Suez Crisis, were fraying. Pearson had turned down LBJ's request for Canadian troops to fight in Vietnam, alongside soldiers from the US, South Korea, Australia, Thailand, and New Zealand. In 1965, while speaking at Temple University in Philadelphia, Pearson said he supported a pause in the American bombing of North Vietnam. His apparent criticism of American foreign policy while he was on American soil enraged the president. The very next day, LBJ grabbed Pearson by the lapels at Camp David, the president's country retreat in Maryland, and shouted "Don't you come into my living room and piss on my rug."

Fortunately for Dad, his gregarious, outgoing manner proved popular and he did what he did best as a reporter, which was make useful contacts that would give him exclusive stories, or at least access to the newsmakers. That skill would have been especially crucial for a foreign correspondent in

Washington. Then, as now, the White House, the State Department, the Commerce Department, and other government agencies largely ignored the foreign press. The news agenda was set by big-city dailies, *The New York Times* and *The Washington Post*, and the main TV networks, ABC, CBS, and NBC. The cable news channels, like CNN, would not appear until the 1980s. If an ambitious foreign correspondent wanted to do more than rewrite the American papers and wire services, he or she had to forge a network of contacts and escape from the Washington bubble as often as possible. My father's easygoing, unpretentious manner, imposing physical presence and alcohol-fuelled gift of the gab smoothed his way. His style was not an act; he was genuinely friendly and adored anyone who was friendly to him. I remember the time he decided to sell his German-built Grundig shortwave radio, which was as big as a small suitcase. He put an ad in the local paper and the first man who arrived to look at the radio hit it off with Dad. The two of them ended up boozing in the front room for hours and when the man left, my father handed back half the purchase price just because they got along so well.

As a kid, I had played "Pee Wee" hockey in Canada, badly, and Dad, foolishly, gave me a chance for redemption in Washington. He enrolled me in a local club and, like all Canadian hockey fathers, rose at dawn to take me to practice during the winters, which were mercifully short by Canadian standards. At one tournament, held in the main arena downtown, I looked up and saw Dad absorbed in conversation with Secretary of Defense Robert McNamara, the driving force behind the Vietnam War between 1965 and 1968. I don't know why LBJ's chief lieutenant was at the rink, but he must have been watching a son or nephew play.

Incredibly, Dad also struck up a friendship with James Jesus Angleton, the CIA's counterintelligence chief from 1954 to 1975. Angleton was convinced the agency had been infiltrated by Soviet moles. How they met, I have no idea, although Angleton would have known about the Gerda Munsinger affair and my father may have used that scoop as his calling card. Dad kept in contact with Angleton after he resigned from the CIA. He would have gone to Angleton's funeral in 1987 had he not been recovering from quadruple bypass heart surgery in Toronto.

My mother embraced the role of foreign correspondent's wife with gusto, throwing terrific Hawaiian-style luau garden parties and formal dinners, one of which was wrecked when Peanuts jumped on the dining room table and dragged the entire roast away. She joined her husband at lavish diplomatic events. We had holidays at the beach in North Carolina and sailed with friends on Chesapeake Bay, where we bought blue crabs by the bushel. Not an extrovert by nature, my mother emerged from her shell and jumped headfirst into the Chevy Chase social aquarium. For the first time in her life, she was genuinely happy and the memories of her terribly sad youth in a dreary northern Ontario mining town must have felt distant, surreal even, as she flounced around in a mini skirt in her glamorous new surroundings. She adored her new friends and the comforts that came with a household supported by a foreign correspondent's salary. Her children ran free and were loved by the neighbours. Her husband was happy, too. But little did she know that he was plotting adventures well beyond the confines of Chevy Chase and Washington.

His trip to Vietnam in the spring of 1967, only nine months after we moved to the United States, was inevitable. By then, the Vietnam War had gone from foreign adventure to American crisis. The mechanized slaughter of innocents, as some viewed it, now appeared nightly on prime-time TV. It was the biggest event on the planet and a test of American resolve to stop the spread of communism. Of course, being Dad, he jumped at the chance to cover his first war, to challenge himself, to ward off boredom, and to see what was really happening on the ground in that enormous and increasingly tragic conflict.

Vietnam is a long, skinny strip of land running 1,625 kilometres from the Chinese frontier in the north to the confluence of the South China Sea and the Gulf of Thailand in the south. It had been a battle zone since the Second World War, when it was the eastern flank of French Indochina, composed of modern-day Vietnam, Laos, and Cambodia. Shortly after Japan invaded north Indochina during the Second World War, Ho Chi Minh, a Vietnamese communist who had been inspired by Soviet Communism, formed the Viet Minh (the League for the Independence of Vietnam) to rid his homeland of both the Japanese occupiers and the often-brutal French colonial administration, which had been in place since the late 1800s.

After Japan's defeat in 1945, the French tried to reassert their influence. But Ho's remarkably fierce army of peasant soldiers gradually took control of the north. The French influence in Vietnam finally ended in May 1954, when the Viet Minh slaughtered the French garrison in the Dien Bien Phu valley, near the Laotian border. This decisive victory sent the world powers scrambling for a peace agreement. They split the country more or less along the 17th Parallel. To the north, there was Ho's communist North Vietnam with Hanoi as its capital. Below was the western-backed South Vietnam, with Saigon as its capital. The two countries were separated by the Demilitarized Zone (DMZ), a strip of no-man's land about 10 kilometres wide that stretched from Laos in the west to the Gulf of Tonkin in the South China Sea.

Vietnam was now divided, but it was not at peace. Viet Minh sponsorship of the Viet Cong in the south ensured the civil war continued. Ultimately, it became a proxy battle ground for the Cold War powers. China and Russia backed North Vietnam's war against the Americans and the South Vietnamese.

The United States, under presidents Dwight D. Eisenhower in the late 1950s, and John F. Kennedy in the early 1960s, fully supported South Vietnam. The Cold War was intensifying and the Americans feared that all of southeast Asia could fall to the communists; this was the "domino theory." It was John F. Kennedy, not his successor, LBJ, who made the first serious troop commitment to South Vietnam. By the end of 1962, some 11,000 American soldiers, called "military advisers," were on the ground, helping the South Vietnamese military fight the Viet Cong. In 1964, the Americans used a minor attack on two US Navy destroyers in the Gulf of Tonkin to justify all-out war against North Vietnam and the Viet Cong.

When my father arrived in Vietnam in 1967, the US Air Force and the Navy were two years into Operation Rolling Thunder, the bombardment of North Vietnam and the longest and most intense aerial attack since the Second World War. At the same time, LBJ was also covertly bombing Laos to cut off communist supply lines into South Vietnam, and was sending shiploads of troops to South Vietnam. The number of American soldiers was approaching half a million.

Dad went to Vietnam thinking the Americans were invincible. He, like so many other reporters, would learn that they had underestimated Ho Chi Minh's will to unite the country. This became glaringly obvious in early 1968, during the Tet Offensive, when sustained attacks by the Viet Cong and the North Vietnamese on American targets brought the war to its bloodiest level.

Back in Chevy Chase, Dad had left a family in discord. He was not ordered to go to Vietnam by his editors in Toronto. He chose to cover a war that could send him home in a box; my mother had absolutely no say in the matter. I doubt the possibility of leaving his children fatherless entered into his calculation. He just went.

The family only learned years later of some of the insane risks he would take to pin down stories, leaving me to wonder if I would, or could, ever match his brazen journalistic prowess.[6] I also now realize that his era was much more free and open, journalistically, than mine and that he took these risks partly because he was allowed to. When I began running around the world in the 1990s and the 2000s, foreign corresponding, especially war reporting, had become a highly managed process. For instance, "embedded" journalists in war zones in the Iraq War, which began in 2003, could go only where the American and British military press handlers allowed them to go, and see what their handlers allowed them to see. Piles of dead bodies were usually excised from the tour. The government had learned its lesson from Vietnam, when horrific shots of death and destruction were instrumental in turning Americans against the apparently senseless bloodshed. When LBJ shocked the world on March 31, 1968 with the announcement that he

---

6 The short answer: I haven't. Though would I, if I'd had the chance? I think so. I have done my fair share of brave, or foolish, things in search of a journalistic authenticity, like night drives looking for refugees and people smugglers along the Libyan border, even though my archetypal North American looks almost scream "kidnap me." And my wife says I'm happiest when I've been teargassed in a riot. I also share Dad's healthy disrespect for status and authority and have collected a few libel suits (all dropped).

would not seek re-election, it was an admission that he had lost the home-front battle to keep the war going. "America's future [was] under challenge right here at home," he said.

Up close and personal was the rule of the day in the 1960s and 1970s. Add in my father's penchant for danger and that style of reporting could become life threatening. By 1967, my mother was used to the idea of Dad taking risks but Vietnam represented a whole new level of danger. It was an all-out war, with no clear front lines, where ambushes were an ever-present threat and where trouble lurked even in seemingly safe spots. Landmines and booby traps, such as sharpened bamboo sticks placed in camouflaged pits, were everywhere. The body count was already high among reporters and photographers. Just before my father left for Saigon, Bernard B. Fall, the prominent French-American journalist and historian who had written a prescient book about America's probable defeat in Vietnam, *Street Without Joy*, was killed when he stepped on a land mine while on manoeuvres with the Marines near Hue, the old imperial capital. His death was widely reported and no doubt rattled my mother.

Mom says she felt sick when Dad said he was going. She knew that he wasn't the type to rewrite US military press releases from the comfort of a Saigon hotel. He would go where the bullets were flying and the bombs were dropping. In an instant, her Chevy Chase happiness turned into dread. When her husband packed up and headed to Dulles International Airport in Virginia for his long flight to Saigon, she feared she would never see him again.

CHAPTER 6

Another Wild Man

NEW YORK, 1998—If I had to pick the precise moment when I knew that, some day, I would make the journey to Vietnam to trace my father's footsteps, it would be the spring of 1998, half a year after I left *The Times* of London to join *The Globe and Mail* in Toronto. I had travelled to Manhattan to meet English war photographer Tim Page, a figure of fascination for me since I first read about him in Michael Herr's *Dispatches*, and I began collecting his photography books after an old girlfriend bought me *Tim Page's NAM*, his gripping photo collection, as a birthday present. Page was one of Herr's beloved "wigged-out crazies running around Vietnam" as a war photographer. He is said to be the model for the frenetic photojournalist played by Dennis Hopper in Francis Ford Coppola's 1979 masterpiece *Apocalypse Now*, whose narration was written by Herr.

War photographers are a special breed. Their role is to capture war as it really is—the violence, the suffering, the action and, yes, even the glamour—and they often die on the job. They take photos of youth shredded alive by enemy gunfire, of the wounded tended by comrades, of destroyed villages and orphaned kids, of acts of heroism, brutality, and compassion. Their role was especially important in Vietnam, where they, like the print and TV reporters, had essentially unlimited freedom to go where they wanted. There was no censorship beyond the military ban on reporting the precise location of US troops and their intended targets. While Vietnam was the first "TV war," the photographers who sold their images to newspapers and magazines around the world also played a crucial role in shaping the public's awareness of the war, and ultimately their revulsion to it. In the 1960s, print was still a powerful medium. And unlike TV images, print images endure. Think of the photograph of Alan Kurdi, the drowned Syrian toddler washed up on a beach in Turkey in 2015. Page would say that "any good picture we did was an anti-war picture."

Some reporters, like my father, doubled up as photographers. Lugging around his bulky Nikkormat camera, the photos he took usually illustrated the articles he wrote. After Dad returned from Vietnam, hundreds of his Vietnam photos, all black and white, ended up in a box that was stashed in the dank basement of the family house in Toronto. I went through them once or twice when I was a teenager and was both fascinated and revolted by the images of the dead and the dying, photos so horrific that they could not be published in a family newspaper. They have since gone missing. I have been looking for them for years and fear they were casually tossed into a garbage bin after a basement flood.

When I met Page in New York, he and the German photojournalist Horst Faas (who died in 2012), had just finished their *Requiem* project, which took the form of a monograph and a travelling exhibit. Twenty years later, I saw it again at the War Remnants Museum in Ho Chi Minh City, the former Saigon. *Requiem* is a collection of photos taken by 135 photographers from all sides, who died covering the war before the fall of Saigon in 1975. The book contains images of Page's two greatest war buddies, Sean Flynn, son of the swashbuckling romantic actor Errol Flynn, and Dana Stone, another American photojournalist hardwired for danger. The pair were last seen alive on April 6, 1970, leaving the Cambodian village of Chi Pou on rented red Honda motorcycles, heading into communist-held territory along Highway 1, not far from the South Vietnam border. Page has been trying to determine their fate and find their remains ever since. He and others believe they were captured by Viet Cong guerrillas and handed over to the Khmer Rouge, the radical communist guerrillas faithful to

Pol Pot, who would become Cambodia's genocidal leader in 1975. They were almost certainly executed.

I spent an afternoon with Page on the Upper East Side's Newseum and was mesmerized not just by the haunting photos, but by Page himself. Page arrived in Vietnam in 1965, at age twenty, and initially shot photos for United Press International. He and his buddies produced some of the greatest war photographs ever, often while doped to the gills. They were addicted to Jimi Hendrix and the Rolling Stones. They rode to assignments on motorcycles and in Huey helicopters. They lived together in Saigon in a building turned social club that was known as Frankie's House, after the resident Vietnamese houseboy.

Page was wounded five times. On August 11, 1966, he nearly bled to death while floating in the South China Sea after the US Coast Guard cutter he was on, the *Point Welcome*, was strafed by three US Air Force fighter-bombers whose pilots had mistaken it for an enemy ship. In April 1969, a hunk of shrapnel from a landmine that exploded three metres in front of him removed twenty cubic centimetres of his brain. By the time he reached the doctors, he'd been written off as dead-on-arrival. But a surgeon found a pulse and during nine hours of surgery pieced his shattered skull back together and saved his life, although several years would pass before he could function normally.

In the Newseum, Page, who was then fifty-four, white-haired, weary eyed and thickening in the middle, gave a small group a tour of the exhibit, picking out the photos that he found especially compelling. "I could go on for hours," he said. "I wish I had a joint and a glass of Sancerre."

At the end of the *Requiem* exhibit tour, I managed to snag a few minutes alone with Page and told him that my father had covered the war in 1967 for the *Toronto Star*. While there is some chance that Page and Dad met each other in Saigon or some hell hole in the field, Page had no recollection of having done so; nor did my father. He asked me if my father had PTSD. I said somewhat, but not crushingly so, adding that the war had haunted him in different ways. "I still have nightmares about the war," he said. "I still have PTSD. Until the mid-seventies, I was living on acid. I had 5,000 hits in the fridge."

I told Page that my father returned from Vietnam in mid-1967, when most Americans thought the war was still winnable, convinced that it was already game over for the mighty US expeditionary forces. Did he feel the same by then? No, he said: "I knew the war would be lost as soon as I got there, in 1965. You can't win wars on body counts. The country was split down the middle in 1954 and the will to have one Vietnam was never going away."

Michael Dugan, a former Douglas A-1 Skyraider ground-attack pilot and later chief of staff of the US Air Force who met my father in South Vietnam, told me the same thing when I tracked him down in 2020. "We ran out of determination," he said. "For us, the war in Vietnam was optional. For the North Vietnamese, the war was anything but."

When I mentioned to Page that I always wanted to retrace my father's journey in Vietnam, he urged me to go. But for a million reasons—career ambitions, marriage, raising two daughters with Karen, moving to the European bureau of *The Globe and Mail* in 2007—it remained an unfulfilled dream until late January 2018, seven years after my father died.

I so regret not having gone while he was still alive, for even as his body wasted away in his final years and the pain set in, his mind and memory were razor sharp. He could have directed me to every spot he visited in Vietnam and brought them to life: the red dirt he flung over his shoulder as he dug a foxhole during a firefight, the smells and noises of the combat bases, the drinks on rooftop bars in Saigon as he watched napalm strikes light up the distant forests, the jolt of the M16 rifle he fired in the chaos of battle to save his life, the roar of the 2,700-hp Skyraider engine as the pilot to his left pulled the plane out of a dive after dropping its bombs.

A month before I finally left for my trip to Vietnam, Page and I had a long Skype call, during which he smoked several joints and gently scolded me after I referred to him as one of my journalistic heroes. "I wasn't a hero and you, Eric, don't need heroes. It was a different era back then and we did what we did because we could," he told me. "What I did was survive and take war pictures." He reminisced nostalgically about the freedom journalists like my father had during the war, which are unimaginable today. "You could wander aimlessly through the country, hitchhiking by plane, by chopper, by boat," he said. "You were entitled to walk into any officers' mess and get decent chow . . . Beautiful women, great food, great dope, great beaches. It's as if the American military let us go feral."

Page and every other reporter I talked to who covered the war says the freedom was intoxicating, and that the "grunts," the soldiers doing the fighting, typically young black and white men from poor families who had no idea why they were sent halfway around the world to kill Vietnamese, felt an affinity for the reporters and photographers. "The average grunt loved reporters," Page told me. "You have to realize that the average age of reporters covering the war was twenty-six. We listened to the same music as the grunts and talked their language. They would pour their hearts out to us. We were all kids, really."

No wonder my father was able to cover so much ground in Vietnam and get such great access. The late Don North, a veteran of fifteen wars who spent a total of five years in Vietnam, some of them as an ABC News correspondent, and who later became a close friend and work colleague of my father, told me over a dinner in Rome shortly before I left for Vietnam in 2018 that covering the war was a thrill. "I remember the feeling of exhilaration of heading back to Saigon after a day running around the field and having a good story. We'd be flying back, with the fresh jungle air coming into the helicopter, skimming over the trees, and it was: 'Wow, what a great job we had!'"

His words called up memories of my father, whose face would light up like a candle when he talked to me about Vietnam. The close calls, the adrenaline rushes, the adventure, the sheer freedom from the daily grind, the journeys into the unknown, living a millimetre, a nanosecond, from death, "like snails on the edge of a razor blade," as Herr put it. Damn, I would think: would I ever feel so alive as he did in those exhilarating moments in foxholes, in firefights, in helicopters?

CHAPTER 7

In His Footsteps

HO CHI MINH CITY, JANUARY 2018—The Hotel Majestic in Ho Chi Minh City, the former Saigon, is a tired but glamorous French colonial pile built in 1925 that, along with the Rex, the Caravelle, and the Continental, was stuffed with journalists, spooks and military types during the Vietnam War years. John F. Kennedy, then a US senator, visited the Majestic in 1951 when the French were still fighting Ho Chi Minh's communist-nationalist forces. Seven decades of colonial rule would not end until the French were thoroughly trounced in the Battle of Dien Bien Phu three years later. Other guests over the years included writer Somerset Maugham, actor Catherine Deneuve, and Graham Greene, author of *The Quiet American*, a prescient tale published in 1955 about misguided American interventionism in Vietnam. Evidently, Kennedy, after he was elected president in 1960, did not take the book to heart. Nor did his successor, LBJ.

It was to the Majestic I headed when I arrived in Ho Chi Minh City on January 29, 2018. The hotel is in the heart of the sprawling, chaotic, traffic-plugged city and faces the muddy brown Saigon River, which was flanked with construction projects and Heineken billboards. At the front desk, I asked if guest records went back to the 1960s, thinking it would be cool to stay in the same room my father did. The receptionist laughed: "That's a long time ago. No computers then."

My room faced the river. Dad may have made the unwise choice of a riverside room on his first nights in Saigon, unaware that seasoned journalists and military officers usually took inside rooms to protect themselves from the rockets fired from the far side of the river by Viet Cong fighters, who were always happy to remind the Americans that they were not safe, even in their adopted fortress city. I ate a quick and delicious Vietnamese street dinner and went to bed, dead tired after my fifteen-hour flight from Rome.

The next day I met Nhung Nguyen, the woman who would be my fixer—guide, interpreter and problem solver—during my whirlwind tour of the spots Dad had visited. Nhung came recommended by an American journalism professor I knew who had met her while researching his books about Vietnam. She was twenty-eight years old, worked as a video journalist, spoke near-perfect English, was addicted to coffee, and had a Zen-like calm about her, all smiles all the time. Whenever I got tense about our inability to find a location on the map I had made of Dad's odyssey, or the right person to interview, she would give me a reassuring look and say, "Everything will be fine."

She was always right. I am sure we looked ridiculous together. I am six-foot-five, a giant by Vietnamese standards; Nhung is five-foot-zero. My adventure would be hers, too. Like many young Vietnamese, she knew that the communists won the "American" war, and that it was also a civil war that killed about two million Vietnamese on both sides, but that was about the extent of her knowledge and she was eager to visit the battle zones that shaped her country.

Whatever she knew about it, Nhung, like all Vietnamese, young and old, had been affected by the war. Her parents were lucky to be alive. They were from a city half way between Hanoi and the port city of Haiphong, the industrial corridor in North Vietnam that was heavily bombed near the end of the American involvement, when Richard Nixon was president. "My parents remember hiding in bunkers when the B-52 bombers came," she told me, referring to the enormous eight-engine Boeing warplanes that could carry more than 50,000 pounds of explosives and strike from such great heights that their presence was often unknown until the blasts opened the ground.

On my second night at the Majestic, I headed to the open-air terrace on the fifth floor, where Dad would have drunk and dined. He told me it was from here that journalists watched American warplanes return to Saigon, occasionally seeing the distant sky turn pink as napalm, jellied gasoline dropped in canisters, incinerated the forest. The Viet Cong were never far away.

It was late and there was only one fellow guest on the terrace, an elderly man with snow-white hair and a friendly demeanour. I suspected he was a US war veteran. He was having a drink and looking out across the river, apparently lost in his memories. I said hello and he invited me to join him. He was Frank Tapparo, eighty years old, from Hershey, Pennsylvania. He was an Army major during the war, working at the Pentagon's Defense Communications Planning Group, "a secret organization," he told me, "that did not exist." And he had stayed at the Majestic whenever he was in Saigon, from 1968 until 1975, when the doomed city fell to the communists and the last Americans were evacuated by helicopter.

The planning group's mission was to line electronic sensors along the Ho Chi Minh trail, the vast logistics network that delivered men and munitions from North into South Vietnam via Cambodia and Laos. Dropped by F-4 Phantom fighter-bombers, the sensors would embed themselves in the ground and detect vibrations made by passing trucks, delivering a radio signal to an overhead electronic-warfare plane, which in turn would call in the bombers from US airbases in eastern Thailand. "Yes, it all worked," Tapparo told me. "But there were so many trucks coming down the Ho Chi Minh Trail all the time, the question was, 'Did we really need these sensors?'"

Tapparo was making his first trip to Vietnam in forty-three years and said he did not recognize the city he had known as Saigon. In the twenty-first century, it was a vast, noisy, skyscraper-studded tangle of some twelve million people and more than eight million scooters flowing through the streets like schools of fish. "I can't believe it," he said. "It looks like Tokyo."

Not that the city was a pretty place during the war. "The leaves were dying on some of the trees," he said. "The soot and exhaust fumes from all the military traffic covered everything. We'd get rocketed a couple of times a week from the swamp across the river. I would always take an interior room for protection."

Still, the modern commercial mess did not displease him. Quite the opposite. The Vietnamese were moving up the value chain as their country turned into an "Asian Tiger" economic powerhouse. The war was long gone and most Vietnamese bore no resentment toward Americans in spite of the near-decade of destruction they inflicted on the country. "I am pleased about what happened here since the war ended," Tapparo said. "I want the best for the Vietnamese people. They were hammered for so long."

I asked him if he had known the Americans would lose the war, and if he thought the media had accelerated that loss. He answered "yes" to both questions, adding: "But the reporters like your father weren't reporting fake news. We had some people who did some bad things here, for sure. I fought an honest war. But it was a war that should never have happened."

He wished me luck on my voyage of discovery, which was about to begin: "You're doing for your dad what I am doing for myself."

CHAPTER 8

The Hill of Angels

THE DEMILITARIZED ZONE, FEBRUARY 2018—About six months before my father died of heart disease, diabetes and who knows what else (he had been a heavy smoker and drinker, and never watched his diet), I asked him to jot down a few notes about his Vietnam experience. He was fading fast and did not get far, leaving me about 1,000 words. Those notes, combined with couple of dozen *Toronto Star* stories, a few of his war photos, my mother's recollections and several serendipitous encounters with war veterans and old war correspondents, were what I had to piece together his journey across Vietnam and within himself.

Bob Reguly did what all good newsmen do when they step off a plane: find the action. Given total freedom to go where they wanted when they wanted, journalists in 'Nam hopped onto planes and helicopters on a moment's notice. And although they were not "embedded," they were usually given the honourary rank of major—field-grade military officer, above the rank of captain, or even colonel if they were big-name bureau chiefs. This gave them access to officers' cots, canteens, and messes (the military argot for dining halls or tents) at US Army or Marine Corps bases. Sometimes they were given rifles and were encouraged to fight when US soldiers were getting gunned down: The boys had more pressing things to do than protect war tourists from the North Vietnamese Army (NVA) and the Viet Cong.

The journalists' freedom in the Vietnam War was extraordinary and no American war, battle, or incursion since then has given the media such hands-off treatment. All reporters had to do was show up at an air base and wait for an empty seat on a helicopter or cargo plane for a flight to wherever they wanted. Given the amount of air traffic (the US military used 12,000 helicopters alone in South Vietnam), they could be aloft within minutes, rarely waiting more than a few hours. Once back on the ground, they could hitch rides on military convoys. If there was space between the ammunition boxes, medics' stretchers, and body bags, they might hop onto a Huey helicopter flight to a combat zone, as long as they were not dressed in colourful civilian clothing, which would make them rather easy targets.

Ray Wilkinson, a British-born former US Marine combat correspondent who I met in Dong Ha in central Vietnam in 2018, where he was working as a volunteer English teacher, told me that the military employed press officers but their main role was to keep journalists alive and point them in the right direction, not censor their articles or restrict their movements. Wilkinson, who fought in, and wrote from, some of the war's biggest battles in 1967 and 1968, including Khe Sanh, Hue, and Con Thien, told me the Pentagon's media policy was rather accidental. "The American military presence in Vietnam was a crawling presence," he said. "Early in the war [1963 to 1965], there were only a few thousand American military advisers in Vietnam, and just a few journalists, and no one paid much attention to them because it was a small war at first. When the build-up happened and a lot more journalists arrived, the Pentagon didn't think it through and just left them without any controls."

Figuring out how to send his stories to his editors in Toronto would have been one of Dad's first priorities after landing. In Saigon, he would have struck a deal with United Press International (UPI) or Associated Press (AP), the two big US news agencies, or Reuters, the British agency, to use their telex system. Telexes were international message-transfer machines that looked like overgrown typewriters. Journalists would write their stories on their portable typewriters, walk or take a taxi to the UPI or AP office, and type them into the telex machine, which would encode the words onto a hole-punched paper tape, similar to a piano roll. Once the line connection was made, the data on the paper tape would be fed into the line and the receiving telex machine would spit out the story. The machines were slow, capable of delivering about sixty words a minute.

The problem came when the journalists were nowhere near a wire-service office. To get a battle-zone story published, they would have to find their way to a combat base away from the fighting, not an easy job if the helicopters and trucks were filled with dead and injured. Hopping a flight to the press centre at a big military base would be the next step. If the press centres did not have telex machines, they would have to wait their turn to use the Americans' main "Tiger" phone network to dictate stories to copy editors on the other side of the planet. The whole process, from fleeing the battle zone to the story's publication in the newspaper, could take a day or two. "Getting a story out was usually the most difficult part of being a journalist in the field in those days," Wilkinson said.

Within two days of arriving in Saigon, Dad had bought his US Army gear on the black market, checked out of the Majestic, and boarded a C-130 Hercules military transport plane to the Phu Bai Combat Base, just south of Hue, the ancient imperial capital on the Perfume River in what is now central Vietnam, then the upper reach of South Vietnam. What he did not know was that he would end up in the Demilitarized Zone (DMZ). Nor did he know that this 10-kilometre-wide no-man's land that separated North and South Vietnam—"the Z" as the soldiers called it—was about to take its place in military history. I will let my father's notes to me pick up the story from here:

When the Herc landed [at Phu Bai], I walked directly to waiting helicopters along with the 700 Marines of the Third [Battalion] of the Fourth Marine Regiment. Only then I was told we would be invading the DMZ.

The Americans claimed that the North Vietnamese were stashing supplies inside the DMZ for smuggling onward to the Saigon area, as rationale for the invasion. We formed a 700-metre perimeter of an elongated U, with the open end smack on the Ben Hai River . . . The temperature was in the 90s.

Four days later there were only 300 of us original 700 left. Most of the casualties were from heavy fire—122-mm Soviet shells that left a hole in which you could bury a small car. The Viets would trundle three or four guns out of the caves, lob several rounds each, and push the guns back in the caves before the US dive-bombers circling above could get a bead on them.

One incident I witnessed: Marine snipers were trying to hit a Viet strapped high in a tree outside the perimeter, obviously radioing corrections to the artillery fire. But he kept ducking behind the trunk. The Americans flew in an Ontos tank in a Chinook copter . . . The Ontos had three 105-mm recoilless rifles on each side of the turret. The Ontos churned up the perimeter, let fly with all six barrels. All that was left was a stump.

At night, there would be an exactly twenty-minute mortar barrage, followed by NVA running through, shooting Kalashnikovs and throwing grenades. In the morning light, there would be bodies from both sides, some still screaming from wounds. There were three run-throughs a night. Each time, I dug my foxhole deeper.

After the first night, a Marine lieutenant told me the NVA can't tell you're a journalist in the dark. So, I got a quick lesson on the M16 [automatic rifle] and used it the next three nights. It was chaos, with everybody shooting, so I never knew whether I killed anybody, but I may have.

My father had unwittingly stepped into Operation Hickory, the first US invasion of the DMZ, which in turn was part of the wider Battle for Con Thien, one of the war's biggest and deadliest running battles. It would not wind down until early 1968.

* * *

My fixer, Nhung, and I met Wilkinson at his hotel in Dong Ha, the rough-hewn city that was home to the northernmost Marine base, and where my father had spent a night or two. Wilkinson fought at Con Thien and wrote stories about it for *Stars and Stripes*, the US military's newspaper, Marine papers, and a few civilian papers. He remembers it being one of the longest and most horrific fights of the war, though one that got less coverage than the Khe Sanh and Hue battles in early 1968, the year after Dad's stint. "Your father's note absolutely rings true," he said. "It was a huge, huge bombardment. It was terrible."

Con Thien, the "Hill of Angels," as local missionaries called it, was a 160-metre-high mound of red clay located about three kilometres south of the DMZ. In 1967, stripped of its forest cover, it was turned into a Marine combat base whose role was to reinforce the McNamara Line, the defensive corridor that stretched along the DMZ from the South China Sea to the Laotian border. Its goal was to prevent the NVA incursions into South Vietnam. Con Thien and Khe Sanh, about 40 kilometres to the southwest, were the main Marine combat bases along the line and both endured long, horrific sieges. Con Thien's value, and vulnerability, was its elevation. From the top of the hill, the Marines had unfettered views across the DMZ and the Ben Hai River that roughly bisected it into North Vietnam. But its location also made it an easy target for NVA shelling. The Marines responded by burrowing into the red soil, building trenches and bunkers, which turned into vats of cold mud during the winter monsoons. Rats and parasites were everywhere and some of the men wore condoms to prevent the leeches from creeping into their urethras while they slept.

The first NVA heavy artillery and rocket attacks began in late February 1967 and intensified from then on. At the time, the hill was defended by the South Vietnamese army, who were replaced by the Marines at the start of May. The NVA shocked the Marines on May 8, when they penetrated the perimeter of the Marines' Con Thien firebase using flamethrowers, rocket-propelled grenades, automatic rifles and Bangalore torpedoes (explosives packed into long pipes that were used to destroy barriers such as barbed wire). Hand-to-hand fighting ensued and the Marines lost forty-four men, with 110 wounded. The Marines had underestimated the fighting strength and skill of the regular North Vietnamese forces. They were not peasant Viet Cong guerrillas in sandals.

Retaliation would come on May 18, when the Marines put a formidable fighting force into action in Operation Hickory, supported by an aerial bombing and ground attack campaign. Hickory was a search-and-destroy mission, designed to trap the NVA troops between two Marine regiments, one advancing north from Con Thien, the other on the Ben Hai River, root out their bunkers and kill as many of them as possible. The battle would finish ten days later, with the Marines taking 142 killed in action (KIA) and almost 900 wounded after running into two well-armed NVA battalions.

The Marines' losses did not end there. Operation Buffalo, the Marine counterattack on the NVA between July 2 and July 14, killed 159 Marines and wounded 345, making it one of their worst disasters of the war. My father's good friend Don North, who covered the Con Thien battle for ABC News shortly after Dad left the area, witnessed the Marines retrieve the bodies after that ambush. In a memoir published in *The New York Times* in July 2017, a year and a half before his death, North wrote: "Many of the [Marine] bodies had been rigged with grenades, and almost all had been mutilated or desecrated. One dead Marine had his genitals cut off and sewn to his face, with a photo of his girlfriend stabbed to his chest."

The Con Thien casualties, and other slaughterhouse battles like it, had a profound effect on the psyche of the American public. They would help put the lie to propaganda that the Americans were on the verge of outright victory. Both North and my father came to that realization after watching the Marines get mowed down at Con Thien.

Reading North's account of Con Thien, which would ultimately kill 1,429 Marines and wound 9,265, and listening to Wilkinson's recollection of the battle, I realized that my father was beyond lucky to have survived the Marine incursion to the Ben Hai River. Wilkinson said Con Thien was a sheer hell: "Everything I saw at Con Thien convinced me it was one of the nastiest battles of the whole Vietnam War. Fighting there reminded me of everything I read about the First World War—the rain, the mud, the trenches, the constant bombardment, the patrols that were terrorized by ambushes."

Dad's story on the DMZ battle appeared on page one of the *Toronto Star* on May 19, 1967, the day after the start of Operation Hickory. Beneath a banner that read "*Star* man goes in with marines," and the headline "U.S. attack takes war to doorstep of N. Viet Nam," lay a story that was not nearly as gripping as the note he would leave me forty years later: The DMZ battle was his maiden assignment in Vietnam, his first battle in his first war, and he had mistakenly taken the intense fighting and shelling as routine, admitting to me in later years that he had "badly underreported that episode."

As far as I could tell from his notes and his published stories, he flew or drove into Con Thien with the 3rd Battalion of the 4th Marine Regiment but actually went into battle on the Ben Hai River with the 2nd Battalion of the 26th Marine Regiment, a unit that fought in the absolutely vicious Battle of Iwo Jima in the Second World War. The battalion was reactivated in Vietnam and would fight at Khe Sanh in 1968, the Vietnam battle that filled America's newspapers and TV screens more than any other. Dad joined them on a resupply helicopter, jerrycans of drinking water on the way in, dead and wounded on the way out. "Two Marines with both legs blown off were loaded aboard," his article read. I imagine they were the first casualties he saw in Vietnam. Within the first thirty-six hours of fighting, the 2/26, as it was known, took 200 casualties.

The *Star* story was full of other horrors. It chronicled the rage of American grunts as "village women came out to strip Marines dead of their watches, canteens, and rain ponchos"; the jolt of watching a soldier as he "jerked with a bullet between the eyes"; the sight of an F-4 Phantom fighter-bomber that pulled up too late and "caromed off a hillside."

And yet, amid the carnage, Dad worked hard to chronicle the humanity that frames all war. "We captured a Viet Cong down south near Chu Lai," he quoted one major as saying. "He took me to his home and showed me a picture of his brother on the wall. The brother was in South Vietnamese uniform."

Years after the war, I asked Dad whether he regretted pulling the trigger when he was in his foxhole. "What was I supposed to do?" he asked me. "What would you have done?"

Wilkinson, whose role as a Marine combat correspondent put him in close contact with civilian war reporters, said he understood why reporters would use weapons. "I would say that 80 per cent of the time, reporters in battle situations did not need to carry a weapon. But Con Thien was different. It was a shit show, every man for himself. I get that your father had to fire his rifle to survive."

At the War Remnants Museum in Ho Chi Minh City a week after I left the DMZ, I visited an exhibit titled, simply, "Requiem." Put together by Tim Page and another legendary war photographer, Germany's Horst Faas, "Requiem" featured pictures shot by photojournalists, on both sides, who died covering the war. One was Sam Castan, a Brooklyn native working for *Look*, the large-format magazine that competed with *Life* magazine. Castan went down fighting in the Central Highlands in May 1966, as he fired a pistol at NVA troops. This is what the former CBS Vietnam War correspondent John Laurence, who wrote Castan's obituary for *Look*, said about him:

> Sam Cast died fighting. He was a civilian journalist who became a warrior in the last minutes of his life—leading a small desperate group of American soldiers out of a trap, saving their lives, losing his own . . . There were no easy choices in Vietnam. Every reporter and photographer who worked in the field worried about this one: What do you do when faced with the likely prospect of death? Pray for a miracle? Fight back? Try to surrender? Die passively?

As I stared at the photos, I better understood why my father and some other journalists sometimes had to battle their way to safety. Dad fought because he was expected to, had to, when the fighting turned against the soldiers who could no longer protect him. He found himself standing alongside those soldiers because, for the most part, he refused to stay with the hotel journalists in Saigon, attending those US press briefings infamous for their inflated enemy body counts and known among reporters as the "Five O'Clock Follies." My father and other correspondents risked their lives in firefights, well aware they could become media martyrs. Because of that, TV screens, newspapers, and magazines in the United States and around the world featured real images of dying soldiers, burnt children, and levelled villages. Journalists delivered those images, and many of them died doing so.

On my journey in 2018, I desperately wanted to visit the area where my father had gone in with the Marines. My goal was to find the spot where he had dug his foxhole ever deeper in the "red gumbo," as he called the muddy soil, to protect himself from the NVA's night time mortar rounds "that had walked through the battalion, wounding scores," and where he was warned not to make his head an easy sniper target by lighting a cigarette. And where he may have killed some NVA soldiers.

I knew he had dug in next to the Ben Hai River and that he thought he was some 80 kilometres from the coast, which seemed to me too far west. That distance would have put him close to the Laotian border, and I know he never made it there. At our hotel in Dong Ha, Nhung and I pored over maps. Wilkinson was staying in the same hotel and was pretty sure the Marines punched into the DMZ to the immediate northwest of Con Thien, which made sense to us and was verified by reports I had read of the battle, including *Hill of Angels*, an engrossing first-hand account of the Con Thien battles by retired Marine Colonel Joseph C. Long.

The next day, we hired a local guide, Nguyen Thi Thanh Hai, and a driver and visited the spooky site of the Battle of Khe Sanh in 1968, which played a big role in Michael Herr's *Dispatches*, then looped back along Highway 9, travelling past other spots that saw fierce fighting—including the Elliot Combat Base (a 240-metre-high hill known as the Rockpile), and Cam Lo, another hellhole my father visited, before swinging north to Con Thien.

Hai explained that we could not actually drive to the Con Thien hill. It was a two-kilometre walk to the site, and there would be nothing to see once we got there beyond some fragments of an old French bunker. So, we headed to the Ben Hai River and found two bridges that lay just north of Con Thien. At that point, we were about 23 kilometres west of the South China Sea. This must have been the spot, or close to it.

One of the bridges was modern and busy with traffic. We took it to the north side of the Ben Hai, where we spotted a footbridge that lay a couple of hundred metres downstream. That is where we headed, crossing to the southern bank of the Ben Hai in what would have been the middle of the DMZ. The river itself was pleasant, its banks covered in lush foliage.

We spotted two fishermen in a small wooden boat, heading slowly upriver, using long poles to propel themselves over the shallows. When we focused on them and the river itself, we had no sense of the modern world, or of a war zone that had absorbed unbelievable amounts of bombs, cannon fire, grenades, bullets, and napalm for two years, turning it into a wasteland soaked in blood, where body counts were sometimes done by counting water canteens, because the corpses were mangled beyond recognition. But the rest of the landscape placed us very much in the twenty-first century. Too much so.

Among the mundane buildings on the top of the river's north side, in what would have been NVA territory, was a karaoke bar whose speakers began blasting away at noon. I told Hai that I wanted to walk along the riverbank, away from the pounding noise, to look for clues of the butchery and chaos my father reported on all those years ago. But my fanciful plan immediately slammed up against the violence that, decades later, still echoes throughout much of Vietnam. Hai glared at me, thrusting her right hand in front of my face. It was covered in scars: shrapnel wounds from a cluster bomb that exploded at her school many years after the war, when she was six. The whole region, she said, is littered with thousands, perhaps hundreds of thousands, of UXOs (unexploded ordnance). Three foreign-funded charities, among them Project Renew, are busy removing them from the bombed-out Quang Tri Province that includes the DMZ area. Dong Ha has a small, chilling museum devoted to the effort. Since the end of the war in 1975, UXOs have killed or injured more than 100,000 Vietnamese.

No, I would not be looking for my father's foxhole. When we left the Ben Hai, I was filled with disappointment, even sadness. I had expected Con Thien and the river to be misty, ghostly, slightly menacing hallowed grounds, where I could imagine the dull whir of helicopter blades, the thud of mortar rounds, and the screams of wounded American and NVA soldiers—the chilling battle sounds my father had heard. Instead, I found a subdivision vibrating to the blare of bad music, its residents happily oblivious to the war. I was happy for them, but I would need to search for Dad's presence elsewhere.

CHAPTER 9

The Imperial Capital Before Its Destruction

CENTRAL VIETNAM, FEBRUARY 2018—After the DMZ, Nhung and I were determined to stick with our plan. We would wind our way south, stopping in as many spots as we could that matched my father's place lines in the *Toronto Star*. Hue was next. And it was a marvel. The imperial capital from the early 1800s until 1945, it is still dominated by the enormous citadel, its menacing two-metre-thick walls facing the Perfume River. Its palaces were home to the Annamite emperors. "Annam" was the name used in the West to refer to Vietnam before it became part of French Indochina in 1887.

Tim Page and Don North had warned me that I would find little visible evidence of the war anywhere in Vietnam, and they were right. Forest and farmland have consumed landing zones and air bases. Some of the house-sized holes left by B-52 bombers are now duck ponds; we saw many of them in Quang Tri Province, just south of the DMZ, which is said to be one of most bombed pieces of real estate on the planet.

In Hue, though, you could still feel the war.

The Battle of Hue, which was the model for the fighting scenes in Stanley Kubrick's 1987 war film *Full Metal Jacket,* was Second World War-style street-to-street combat. Among the longest battles of the war, it began on January 31, 1968, the day after the start of the Tet Offensive, when some 80,000 NVA and the Viet Cong fighters attacked more than a hundred towns and cities in South Vietnam in an attempt to break the morale of the American and South Vietnamese troops and trigger a popular uprising that would bring down the Saigon government. The assault on Hue was one of the nastiest battles of the Tet Offensive. It levelled the city by the time it was over in early March. We saw bullet holes and shattered walls in the citadel and what was left of the imperial palaces. Our visit on a leaden, wet day, reinforced Hue's sinister aura.

My father arrived in Hue half a year before the big battle, and his *Star* stories from here, by turns funny and disturbing, comprised vignettes of life in wartime. In one, he wrote about two French-speaking priests who drove over a small landmine that wrecked their jeep, but left them only slightly wounded. The next day, the Viet Cong tracked them down and demanded payment for the mine, which was meant for American military vehicles, not civilian jeeps. "The priests paid. Non-payment meant execution," my father wrote. Dad may have been the last journalist they met. When the Viet Cong infiltrated the largely undefended city in late January, they rounded up anyone deemed to be anti-communist, "reactionary" elements, including foreigners, aid workers, missionaries, Christian clerics, and South Vietnamese government and civilian officials who worked for the US or South Vietnamese military, and executed them. The mass killings were not uncovered until after the war. Two of the victims were Fathers Urbain David and Guy de Compiegne, whose bodies were found by Benedictine monks in a shallow grave a few months after the Battle of Hue. My father did not name the priests in his jeep vignette, and there could not have been many French-speaking priests in Hue, a small city, in 1967.

In another article, he interviewed an American pilot from the nearby Phu Bai combat base who had made a low-level strafing mission over a field when a Viet Cong fighter stood up and hurled rocks at the plane. He quoted the pilot: "I made another pass and let go at him with my rockets and guns. His head went sailing over my canopy." As proof, the pilot produced photos of the event taken by the plane's automatic gun-camera.

The next byline came from Quang Ngai, about 200 kilometres south of Hue, where Dad interviewed a Canadian-Dutch doctor who was treating civilian war victims. He was Alje Vennema, the McGill University medical graduate who was director of Canadian medical assistance in Vietnam from 1965 to 1968. For his selfless work, Vennema received the Order of Canada in 1967. The story was long and moving, but for me, its value lay in its strong anti-war tone. Already, Dad was realizing the war was an unwinnable outrage. Among other horrors, the article talked about three children killed by an American blast, their bodies swollen by the concussion. He quoted the doctor: "Is it any wonder the people hate the Americans? The people see this war as white men killing Asians. The Americans can't win. If I had my way, they would pull out by eight o'clock tomorrow morning."

The good doctor was lucky to survive the war. He was in Hue during the Tet Offensive, saw the Viet Cong drag away civilians to be executed, and found their bodies after the Viet Cong and the NVA were driven out of the shattered city. In his 1976 book about the atrocity, *The Viet Cong Massacre at Hue*, he listed twenty grave sites that contained 2,400 bodies. I remember my father talking about Vennema's bravery and compassion and I imagine they kept in touch after the war. He died in British Columbia in 2011, within months of my father's death.

On our last night in Hue, Ray Wilkinson drove down from Dong Ha and joined Nhung and me for dinner at the elegant Azerai La Residence hotel, a rare moment of luxury for us during our rather uncomfortable backroads odyssey. La Residence is located on Le Loi street, parallel to the Perfume River, and was the scene of vicious building-to-building fighting. "This so freaks me out," he told us as we drank expensive French red wine. "I fought along this street, Le Loi street, and now I am in a five-star hotel having a lovely meal here. Who would have thought?"

CHAPTER 10

The Bombing Mission

PLEIKU, VIETNAM, FEBRUARY 2018—The Douglas A-1 Skyraider was a brute of a plane, designed late in the Second World War to chop its way through the air, and already an anachronism by the Vietnam War. In an era of supersonic jets, it employed a thundering eighteen-cylinder piston engine. Its chief value was its ability to fly low and slow, picking out targets that the jet would miss. It could stay aloft for hours, often circling and protecting downed pilots until the rescue helicopters arrived. The US Air Force and the Navy lost 266 Skyraiders in Southeast Asia, and 144 pilots. It was a widow-maker. Anyone who chose to fly it was, by definition, brave, perhaps stupidly so. Yet it was also lauded as the most effective ground-attack plane of the Vietnam War, maybe of all-time, and its pilots adored the machine they called "Spad," after the First World War French biplane that was used by America's first combat pilots in 1917 and 1918.

My father would go on a Skyraider mission in June 1967, out of Pleiku, the main city in the Central Highlands, just east of Cambodia, and home of a big US Air Force (USAF) base. "Anything for a story," he wrote to me.

Nhung and I arrived in Pleiku after a bouncy, eight-hour trip from the coast in a Toyota SUV that took us along parts of the Ho Chi Minh Trail. We rolled past waterfalls, and forests mutilated by illegal logging. The trip was a slog. We had two drivers, who changed places every hour or so, and the heat was intense. My father flew his Skyraider mission over this rugged landscape.

His plane, which took to the sky alongside another Skyraider, was piloted by Captain James (Jimmy) Reed Thyng, whose personal insignia, a lucky shamrock, was stencilled onto both sides of the camouflaged fuselage. Below each shamrock was "Gigi," the nickname of his then-wife, Georgette. A few weeks before I left for Vietnam, I endeavoured to find out what happened to Thyng. Maybe he did not survive the war; if he did, maybe he was still around and remembered Dad.

Given the high mortality rate among Skyraider pilots, and the half century that had passed since the war, I did not get my hopes up. But thanks to the Internet, I found him in Pittsfield, New Hampshire, his hometown. He was seventy-six in 2018. He told me on the phone that he had a heart problem, but was otherwise well, and was worried about his later wife, Marilyn, who was suffering from breast cancer. Incredibly, he remembered my father. "Your dad was courageous," he said, a far cry from a particularly nervous Australian journalist he once took aloft: "He carried three canteens, one water, two vodka."

Thyng fascinated me and we talked often over the next couple of years, sometimes for hours at a time. My father was lucky. Thyng was one of the ablest combat pilots of the Vietnam War, and was the son of Harrison Thyng, a legendary fighter pilot who flew in the Second World War and the Korean War. The more I talked to Jimmy Thyng, the more I came to realize that while we were two very different people, we had one crucial thing in common: the domineering and influential father figure.

Harrison, or Harry, Thyng was small but fearless, with a .38-calibre pistol on his hip, gunslinger style. He was one of only seven American pilots who was an ace in both conflicts in propeller and jet aircraft. Among American military pilots, ace status is acquired with five or more confirmed kills. Born in New Hampshire in 1918, he fell in love with flying and was shipped to England in 1942, where he flew British Spitfires with the US Army Air Force's 309th Fighter Squadron of the 31st Fighter Group, the first American squadron to see combat in the European theatre. On August 8,

1942, while flying a Mark V Spitfire, he damaged a German Focke-Wulf Fw 190 fighter, a superior aircraft, handing him the first combat claim against a Luftwaffe aircraft by an American pilot in the war. His greatest success came after he was transferred in late 1942 to North Africa, where the Allies were fighting Vichy French and German forces. He was shot down twice, once by ground fire behind enemy lines and once by British anti-aircraft gunners, who mistook his Spitfire for an enemy aircraft. In North Africa, he was officially credited with five aircraft kills, though his son told me the true figure was seven. In May 1945, three months before the Americans dropped the first atomic bomb on Japan, he was transferred to the Pacific and claimed he shot down one Japanese fighter, although he was not credited with that kill. He also witnessed the atomic bomb drop on Nagasaki on August 9. In 1951, he was sent to Korea, where he flew F-86 Sabres, one of the first jet fighters, and shot down seven enemy MiG-15 jets. In 1966, the same year his boy arrived, Harrison flew a few surveillance missions in Vietnam to assess the enemy air threat. He retired as a highly decorated brigadier general later that year and died in 1983 at age sixty-five. A white granite monument to his flying success was erected in Pittsfield in 2004 and is considered a holy spot by fans of fighter aces.

So Jimmy Thyng and I were both sons of highly successful, overpowering men who we worshipped and who utterly shaped our lives. Both of us had followed in our father's professional footsteps, me to the point that I felt competitive with him and judged by him. And, like Thyng, I never thought I could match my father's feats. "I revere my father as a hero," Jimmy told me. "But I held up his accomplishments as things that I could never achieve myself."

You and I get each other, I thought. And we were both right. Neither of us have achieved the fame our fathers found.

Although Jimmy Thyng was being modest. He had inherited his father's boyish enthusiasm for flying, and it was Harry who taught him his craft, when he was only fifteen, in a little Aeronca Champion two-seater. But he also inherited his father's bravery. I found a Skyraider training class photo on an Internet military site, taken at the USAF's Hurlburt Field training site in northern Florida in mid-1966, a few months before Jimmy shipped off to Vietnam. The black and white photo shows eleven men in flight uniform in front of the menacing bulk of a Skyraider. The men are dwarfed by the plane's enormous four-blade propeller. Thyng, kneeling in the front row and sporting a moustache, was the only one of them who was smiling—beaming, actually, as if he could not wait to jump back in the cockpit and ram the throttle forward. The others had stern, even worried, looks on their faces. Maybe they were dreading going to a war that was, by then, already massacring Skyraiders in alarming numbers. Two of the eleven men in his training class would be killed in action in Vietnam. The remains of one of them, Captain Darrell Spinler, lost in a Skyraider mission over Laos on June 21, 1967, the very week that my father visited the Pleiku air base, were not found until 2010.

Captain Jimmy Thyng flew 301 missions in 1966 and 1967 with the USAF's 1st Air Commando Squadron, including twenty combat sorties over North Vietnam, the most dangerous missions. His plane got hit forty-three times, an average of once every seven flights. In one mission, the ground crew counted 288 holes in his Skyraider, the result of a freak mishap. Ground fire hit a cluster bomb unit hanging below his wing, which detonated, nearly shredding the plane. "All the holes were from my own ordinance," he said. "But she got me home. That's how tough those Skyraiders were."

The mission that came closest to ending his life was when he was escorting Fairchild C-123 Providers, twin-engine military cargo planes, which were spraying highly toxic and carcinogenic Agent Orange defoliant over the Ho Chi Minh Trail in Laos, a "crop-dusting" flight, to use the cynical argot of the pilots. They were flying low and Thyng's Skyraider got hit by 37-mm cannon fire that "blew the belly out of my plane." That was just the start. Bullet fire blasted his cockpit canopy, sending a piece of shrapnel into his shoulder. At the same time, the Skyraider engine took seven rounds from a heavy machine gun, knocking out two of the eighteen cylinders. With the engine smoking and off balance, the plane shook violently. Against all odds, he nursed the crippled plane home, thinking it would break into pieces at any moment, and landed safely. The ground crew was astonished that Thyng survived. He emerged from the cockpit bleeding, his flight suit stained red, and the plane was a write-off. "I didn't have time to be scared," he said. "I just had to think about getting that Spad home."

He was awarded the Purple Heart, the medal given in the name of the president for soldiers wounded or killed in action. "No one ever wants to win a Purple Heart," Thyng told me.

* * *

Dad arrived at Pleiku Air Base in the third week of June 1967, when the number of American troops in Vietnam had reached half a million, almost full fighting strength. It was also when the first of the mass anti-war protests turned the centres of Washington DC, New York, San Francisco, and a few other big cities into battle zones between police and protestors. He talked his way onto a bombing mission and Thyng agreed to take him up. There was no formal protocol, no pleading with military press officers, no training—unimaginable in the twenty-first century. He just grabbed a parachute and followed Thyng onto the tarmac as his Skyraider, built in 1952, tail number EC 883, in mottled brown and green camouflage, was loaded with bombs and bullets. The Skyraider could carry its own weight in ordinance, making it a formidable ground-attack weapon. Thyng sat in the pilot's seat on the left side of the cockpit. Dad was on the right, wearing a flight helmet connected to the cockpit intercom, their knees narrowly separated by a console that contained the radio equipment, power-failure warning lights, and various switches. They sat on their parachutes. As a former Smokejumper, my father would not have needed a lesson on pulling a ripcord and certainly knew more about free-fall jumps than Thyng. There were no ejection seats. If they needed to bail out, they would have to climb down onto the wing and leap.

Dad would have been well aware by then of the Skyraiders' high loss rates. But Thyng told me that he got zero sense that the Canadian reporter was nervous. The four or five other journalists he had taken up in previous sorties were terrified, he said: "Your dad carried about him an air of confidence, an I-can-do-this attitude. I didn't have to calm him down. He just popped into his seat and said, 'Let's do this!'"

Skyraiders hunted in pairs. Dad was not allowed to touch anything in the cockpit but staying put delivered plenty of drama on its own. Spotting a single thatched hut, perhaps an ammunition dump, Thyng proceeded to deliver the all-American wipe-out treatment. My father, wrote in the *Star*: "[O]ur Skyraider plummeted into a 60-degree dive from 5,000 feet, dropped two bombs from 2,000 feet, pulled up sharply at 1,000 feet, the 2700-hp engine clawing for sky . . . [We] made four dives, pulling out with a fake left and climbing off to the right. Each plane alternated passes— 'so the enemy doesn't know what's coming next,' pilot Thyng said in the intercom."

The two planes then circled around for a strafing that did not produce a secondary explosion. The hut probably had not been hiding ammo. "After the landing back in Pleiku, Captain Thyng was slightly apologetic over the mission," Dad's story read, "saying they're often much more interesting." Thyng told my father about the rare times he saw the Viet Cong in action. "I once caught some VC out in the open and killed 25 of them with my cannon. Another time a [US] convoy was ambushed. The VC were climbing all over the buttoned-up tanks trying to get in with explosives. We had to strafe the tanks to get them off."

When Thyng and my father landed back in Pleiku, there was a surprise for them in the form of Mike Dugan, a fellow Skyraider pilot from Albany, New York, who was thirty and had been shot down the night before over Laos, near the Ho Chi Minh Trail. Dad had a few paragraphs about his near-miraculous survival in the story he wrote about his Skyraider ride and I was able to flesh out the details in a long phone call with Dugan fifty-three years later. Thyng remembered my father talking to Dugan for an hour or longer, although Dugan himself had only vague memories of meeting the chatterbox Canadian journalist who was obviously infatuated with the mission that almost killed him.

Dugan and three other Skyraider pilots were on an early evening mission over the Mu Gia Pass, on the border of North Vietnam and Laos, a critical supply route to the Ho Chi Minh Trail that was bombed into moonscape throughout the war. They were dropping gravel mines, small mines that were camouflaged to look like rocks or leaves, at low altitude. When he was only 60 or 70 metres over the forest, ground fire blew off his plane's left wing. The Skyraider immediately flipped over and fell. Dugan was upside down. He slammed the canopy open and the negative g-forces sucked him out as he pulled his parachute ripcord. It would be the last recorded bailout without an ejection seat in USAF fighter history. After he hit the ground, he hid his parachute under foliage and looked for spot to hide himself, one that was close to a clearing that could serve as a rescue helicopter pickup landing spot, if he survived the night. "At one point, I heard some enemy troops," Dugan told me. "They got so close that I could smell them, the smell of guys who had lived in the jungle for a month. That was a significant opportunity for me not to sneeze, not to budge."

At dawn, he heard the fleet of aircraft that had been sent from a base in Thailand to rescue him, eight Skyraiders, and a Sikorsky HH-3E, a long-range search and rescue helicopter that was known as the "Jolly Green Giant." Dugan pulled out his survival radio to let the pilots know he was alive and released a purple smoke flare. Of course, the radio signal and the flare would alert the North Vietnamese soldiers. He figured he had maybe four or five minutes to get rescued or face almost certain death. As the Skyraiders laced the forest around him with "suppression" cannon fire, he ran to the clearing and was hoisted to safety with enemy guns crackling nearby. A few hours later, he was back in Pleiku, where his fellow pilots and my father were astonished to see him walk into the mess hall. Dad relished the story. He quoted Dugan as saying: "The patrols looking for me came within 10 feet. The NVA patrol leader smoked a stinking cigar and it almost made me cough."

Thyng flew his last combat sortie in August 1967, two months after Dad flew with him. He was told he could go home early after his twentieth mission over North Vietnam. It was close to miraculous that he was still alive, given that he had flown into danger almost every day since his arrival eleven months earlier, and his commanders thought it best not to allow him to push his luck. To speed up his repatriation, his buddies placed him in a wheelchair even though he was in robust good health, because the "wounded" were given flight priority. The ruse worked and he returned to New Hampshire to see his wife and two daughters, one of whom was born after he left for Vietnam. "I never flew the A-1 Skyraider again," he told me. "Though to this day, I think of her in my dreams quite often. She was my lover, next to my wife."

Thyng made it clear to me that he was a hawk who thought the Americans lost the war because they did not invade North Vietnam; did not level Hanoi and Haiphong, the main port and industrial city in North Vietnam; did not go on dam-busting raids that could have flooded the rice fields and triggered a starvation crisis. "I was feeling, what the hell are we doing here if they don't let us fight the war?" he said.

Dugan, who retired as a four-star general, had a similar take on the war when we talked by phone from his home in Colorado. "If you want to defeat an enemy, you have to do so where the enemy lives," he said. "If we wanted to defeat North Vietnam, we should have done so in North Vietnam."

He does not believe the theory that the media lost the war for the United States, even if an endless stream of articles and images of bloodshed horrified millions of Americans. "Journalists like your father came to Vietnam as professionals," he said. "They just wanted to see what was going on. I don't think they went there to automatically oppose the war. Today, it's so different. Journalists all have an agenda. Not the ones I met in Vietnam."

I do not agree or disagree with Dugan or Thyng. Even if I thought the war was hideously immoral, would it have been any less or more immoral if North Vietnam had been obliterated, handing the United States a victory? My only agenda during my trip to Vietnam was to recreate my father's journey, to visit the exact spots where he endangered his life for journalism, and to see if I could detect his ghostly presence in a country that was burying its savagely violent past as it evolved into an Asian economic powerhouse.

Nhung and I went to Thyng's and Dugan's Pleiku Air Base. It was easy to find. It had been converted into the city's modern airport with the same footprint. We could not find a trace of the old field, even though it was vast. I was disappointed. I had wanted to imagine my father roaring along a dusty airstrip as Thyng took him aloft in their Skyraider. I had wanted to send a photo of an old Skyraider hangar or another war relic to Thyng, who never returned to Vietnam after the war. For all the missions he flew, for all the comrades he lost, there was only defeat, symbolized by the total eradication of the American presence there.

Instead, I sent him a photo of me standing in front of a Skyraider at the War Remnants Museum in Saigon that I visited a few days later, and he was thrilled. The plane was captured by the communists after the city was overrun by North Vietnamese troops in April 1975. It still carried its USAF markings and camouflage paint job, virtually identical to that of Thyng's plane. I spent half an hour staring at the killing machine that so terrified the Viet Cong and North Vietnamese fighters, circling it, running my hands over its aluminum skin and heavy black propeller, marvelling at its bulk and menacing, if inelegant, appearance. I looked up at the cockpit and wondered if I would have been able to climb aboard with Thyng. Perhaps, but not with my father's cool composure. His motto was "show no fear."

CHAPTER 11

My Father's Ghost

PLEI BENG, CENTRAL HIGHLANDS, *February 2018*—On June 12, 1967, the *Star* published a story under the headline "Moving Day for the Montagnards Meant Helicopters at Gunpoint," next to a shot of my father in army fatigues. It included two photos taken by him. One was of a CH-47 Chinook heavy-lift helicopter hovering over the village of Plei Beng; the other showed a young man in a loincloth, with a tethered goat at his feet, waiting for the airlift. He looks perplexed.

What my father bore witness to that day was the forced relocation of Montagnard tribespeople in Vietnam's Central Highlands, southwest of Pleiku, near one of the main branches of the Ho Chi Minh Trail, just east of the Cambodian border. Montagnard is French for "people of the mountain," a catch-all term that an anthropologist would find largely meaningless: the Montagnards are composed of many minority ethnic groups, each with its own language and customs. During the war, the Americans turned millions of South Vietnamese into refugees in their own county, moving them into "strategic hamlets" protected (often badly) by US and South Vietnamese troops. The idea was to remove the hamlets from the influence of the Viet Cong. The effect was to turn their previous homelands into wholesale killing zones under the assumption that anyone who stayed behind was the enemy. The program alienated the South Vietnamese peasants and was officially disbanded fairly early in the war. But it would live on in other guises, and it swept through the Montagnard areas.

The Montagnards were an agrarian tribal people, living in thatched huts. The men wore loincloths; the women were bare-breasted. Some were Christian, other practised animism. Many of their men were hired as mercenaries by the US Special Forces, the Green Berets. They fought well and were later punished by the conquering communist forces for having picked the losing side of the war. Many Montagnard villages were burned; their lands colonized. There are credible reports that thousands were killed in the post-war years.

Almost half a century after the capitulation of South Vietnam, relations between the Montagnard peoples and the "lowland" Vietnamese remain tense. About a decade before my arrival, some of the Montagnards had staged an uprising, demanding religious freedom and the return of their ancestral lands. They were swiftly supressed, and the Vietnamese military keeps a close eye on the region.

Here are excerpts from my father's story that day in June:

The 422 Montagnard villagers scratched themselves awake at dawn to find 150 US infantry men surrounding them. . .

Then they hunkered down to await the twin-rotored Chinook helicopters that would take them away to the giant resettlement camp 12 miles away. . .

The idea is to move about 10,000 Montagnards into one massive tin-roofed Levittown guarded by 1,000 Vietnamese troops. This would turn a 400-square-mile area in the Central Highlands into a "free fire zone," where anything that moves would be regarded as the enemy. . .

The rush program, at the start of the six-month highland monsoon season, would allow unrestrained use of overwhelming American firepower to counter the expected North Vietnamese Army attacks that would come with the cover of heavy rain.

Plei Beng, explained the American officer directing the evacuation, was regarded as a "hostile village." He said the North Vietnamese came in every eight days to collect rice and cart off a few young men to dig bunkers in the surrounding hills. . .

Everything went aboard [the helicopters] but the cows. These were herded down the road to be trucked to the resettlement camp. So honest are these Montagnards that they refused to take along five of the cows, saying that no one in the village owned them, that they had just wandered in.

At 5 p.m., the last chopper-load whirled aloft, leaving the troops to burn down the village with thermite grenades, gasoline and matches.

No wonder the Americans could not win, I thought as I read and reread the story. They could not make friends anywhere.

Plei Beng did not exist on any map I found. Did the Montagnards return to the village after the war? I did not know. But I did know that I wanted to find the spot where my father had documented its eradication. The only clue I could find came from the website of Peter G. Bourne, an expert in combat stress who spent a year in Vietnam as head of the US Army's Psychiatric Research Team. He would later have a distinguished career in academia, government (as US president Jimmy Carter's drug czar in the late 1970s), and at the UN where he was a top health official. Early in the war, in 1965 or 1966, he joined a combat patrol to capture an "enemy village" in the Central Highlands and wrote an elegant, harrowing essay of the experience, "The Road to Plei Beng," published on his personal website.

Bourne's special forces team, along with seventy-five Montagnard mercenaries and twenty-five undisciplined and ill-tempered South Vietnamese soldiers, traipsed through thick forest and elephant grass for almost a full day to reach Plei Beng, which they believed was a Viet Cong stronghold. They ambushed the village, destroyed it without resistance, and airlifted the survivors, mostly women and children, to their base camp. He remembered an old lady making him tea in her house before the soldiers burned it down. Bourne, like my father after him, was deeply saddened by the experience of having seen the destruction of a village full of poor, illiterate peasants. Had it really been a Viet Cong stronghold? After the survivors were relocated, Bourne said he would spend many hours with them, "consumed by my own personal guilt," and that his time in Vietnam left him "cynical, callous and disillusioned but strikingly better informed, more worldly and confident in who I was and what I believed." I am convinced my father went through the same process.

Plei Beng was obviously resettled at some point after the destruction witnessed by Bourne. In June 1967, the village was back on the US military's to-do list and Dad was there to see its second eradication from the map. Bourne put the village "northwest of our camp, Duc Co, only a few minutes away by helicopter but nearly 24 hours' march through the jungle." Duc Co we found: it was a special forces camp best known for the 1965 baptism by fire of (Stormin') Norman Schwarzkopf, famous for leading the coalition forces in the 1991 Gulf War. We found the old runway, now nothing more than a level expanse of red dirt. As we drove, Nhung suddenly found a "Beng" with her maps app. It was only a few kilometres from Duc Co. That must be it, we thought. And it was.

Beng was a hardscrabble village, a hamlet really, about an hour's drive southwest of Pleiku. There were a couple of dozen simple houses on either side of a partly paved road, many with chickens and pigs running around outside. We found a small general store and, oddly, an outdoor beauty parlour where a young woman, all smiles, was cutting a client's hair. It was surrounded by cashew and rubber trees planted in copper-coloured soil. Clay pots for collecting latex from the rubber trees were piled up everywhere, and raw cashews were drying on bamboo mats in the sun.

Our driver from Pleiku, Minh, told us that this part of Montagnard country was inhabited by the Jarai people, whose traditional religion is animism and whose tombs are small huts that contain a few of the deceased's possessions. Few foreigners come to Beng, in part because it's a "restricted" area; we were supposed to have military clearance to be there. We asked a woman walking along the road if she could introduce us to the oldest people in the village, and soon we meet Roh Cham Chich, who said he was age eleven and living in a nearby hamlet in 1967. He looked younger than his age and was wearing a grey T-shirt. His belt buckle was decorated with the logo of the Communist Party. He did not recall the American helicopters but did remember US trucks rolling back and forth, probably carrying the Montagnards' livestock to their new homes. "Only half of the Montagnards agreed to get evacuated," he told us. "The ones who didn't would go to Cambodia and join the North Vietnam forces."

As Minh, ever more agitated, urged us to leave before the military showed up to ask difficult questions, we spotted an old man, hunched, moving slowly toward his sturdy flat-roofed house, which was painted a pleasing light green. He was thin and wore a baseball cap and a stained sweater that was one shade darker than the soil. He had a gentle, if distant, air about him. His eyes were sad and his voice was very soft; his daughter explained that he was not well and had little energy. Bending over to steady himself, he struggled up the three front steps to his house and shuffled to the edge of his wooden bed, no mattress, which faced outdoors, and sat down.

Nhung and I followed him inside. His bedroom was simple and clean. The walls were bare, although their lower third, oddly, was decorated with a painted geometric frieze that looked as if it was inspired by an ancient Roman villa. Beneath his bed was a rounded and dented green metal bucket that looked suspiciously like the iconic American M1 combat helmets used in the war, and probably was.

Kpuih Doan, now almost eighty years old, had been in Beng, then known as Plei Beng, during the evacuation. His daughter said he collected scrap metal after the war, no doubt from American bombs, which meant he was probably exposed to chemicals that could have damaged his brain and nervous system. I wondered if his exposure to the chemicals explained why he had trouble speaking. I handed him a copy of my father's story and he looked intently at the photo of the Chinook helicopter hovering over the village—his village—spreading dust over the thatched-roof huts as twenty or so Montagnards huddled on the side of the landing zone, surrounded by baskets stuffed with their meagre belongings. His eyes lit up. "Yes, I remember the helicopters like this," he said, softly. "I remember collecting our belongings."

I figured he would have been about twenty-eight years old at the time. He stared at the photo again and went quiet. He was either exhausted or absorbed by flickering images of swirling helicopter blades and screaming soldiers with guns, I could not tell. He gave me a weak smile as he clutched the newspaper story. At that instant, I felt certain that my father saw this man, maybe even met him or photographed him, on that hot, frightening day in June 1967.

You are part of my father's history, I thought, and now mine.

I wanted to stay with Doan. I wanted to give him time to see if any other memories of that day trickled back while I studied his face for clues. But Minh hustled Nhung and me into the Toyota for fear the police or soldiers would find us. He took a backroad that steered us well clear of the military outpost we had spotted on the way in. As we bounced along the broken roads to Pleiku, I was buzzing. Finally, I had felt my father's presence in Vietnam. I felt spiritually closer to him in those precious moments than at any time since his death eight years earlier.

Bob getting ready for a parachute training jump, probably 1952. Location unknown, but possibly Kitchener, Ontario, airport, where he learned stunt jumping to earn beer money during his days at the University of Western Ontario.

Bob, far left, with his Saskatchewan Smokejumper crew, summer 1953. Note the knives fastened to the front of the reserve chute. They were used to cut the chute lines if the jumpers got trapped in trees on their descent.

Bob and Ada Reguly in the kitchen of their home in Ottawa, 1960, when he was a member of the *Toronto Star*'s parliament bureau, his first posting beyond the head office.

In the *Toronto Star* newsroom, late 1950s or early 1960s.

With his three children in their church-going splendor in a neighbor's garden in Chevy Chase, Maryland, 1967 or 1968. He is holding Rebecca; Susan and I are standing.

A day or two after Bob's return from Vietnam in the summer of 1967, standing at a wharf in San Francisco in a bespoke silk suit he bought during a layover in Hong Kong. Just the week before, he was in a war zone.

In the *Toronto Star* newsroom, just before he moved to the Washington DC bureau.

Bob's own photo of the forced evacuation by US Army helicopters of the inhabitants of the Montagnard village of Plei Beng, near the Cambodian border, in June 1967. The villagers were removed to make the area a free-fire zone on the assumption that anyone who remained was Viet Cong.

[Right] Ada at a hotel in Miami Beach, Florida, in August 1968. She joined Bob when he was covering the Republican National Convention.

[Left] Bob during the Vietnam War, spring 1967, location unknown but likely at the Ben Hai River in the DMZ. This shot was used as his photo byline for his *Toronto Star* combat stories.

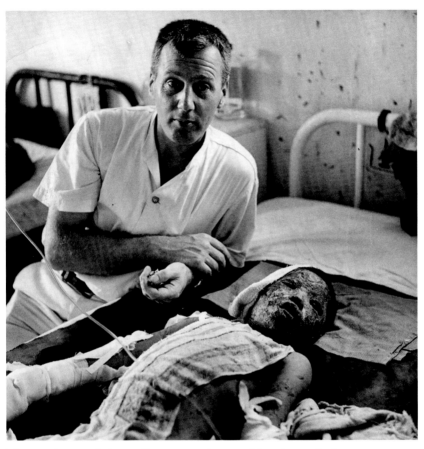

The Canadian-Dutch doctor Alje Vennema, director of Canadian medical assistance in Vietnam from 1965 to 1968. He is in a Quang Ngai medical ward, attending to a child burnt by American napalm.

Bob on a runway in Biafra, the breakaway Nigerian province, in early 1970, during the last stages of the Nigerian Civil War.

CHAPTER 12

Retreat From Vietnam

HO CHI MINH CITY, Late February 2018—Looking at the pink dots on my Vietnam map when I got back to the Hotel Majestic near the end of our whirlwind tour, I realized that Nhung and I had visited no more than half of the locations my father covered as he brought the reality of war home to North American readers.

Among the sites we had to forgo was Rach Kien, a village about 20 kilometres southwest of Saigon, in the Mekong Delta, where he went aloft in a Cessna O-1 Bird Dog, a small, single-engine Cessna observation plane with two seats. That mission's purpose was to spot suspected Viet Cong hamlets and mark them with smoke grenades and white-phosphorous rockets, after which the F-100 Super Sabre jets circling overhead would swoop in with high-explosive bombs, napalm, and 20mm cannon fire. One hamlet was eradicated as my father and the Bird Dog pilot, Paul Sullivan, watched the explosions. "Thanks for coming down," Sullivan told the Super Sabre pilots, one of whom responded: "Rodge [Roger]. Thank you. We enjoyed it."

Oh, the casual brutality of war.

Another spot we did not have time to visit was Landing Zone Two Bits, or what was left of it. Two Bits was a combat base used by the Americans and the South Vietnamese in 1967. It was located at the southern edge of the An Lao Valley, near the South Vietnam coast, about 650 kilometres north of Saigon. It was home to the 1st Cavalry Division, better known as the Air Cav, the US Army's air assault force that began life as a horseback cavalry division and was one of the most highly decorated combat units of the Vietnam War. In modern culture, the Air Cav achieved fame in the movie *Apocalypse Now,* when Huey helicopters under the command of the mad colonel played by Robert Duvall ("I love the smell of napalm in the morning") enthusiastically destroyed a coastal Viet Cong village, then sent his boys surfing. When Dad was at Two Bits, the Air Cav was equipped with 16,000 men and 460 helicopters and its casualty rate was high. By the time war ended, 5,444 of its men had been killed in action and 25,592 wounded.

My father went on a mission with the Air Cav in late June 1967, one that was potentially far more dangerous than the Skyraider bombing mission with Jimmy Thyng a month earlier. Riding at only 30 metres off the ground in a Huey gunship helicopter, their mission was a "hare-and-hounds game," as Dad put it in his article. Soldiers would drop vomiting-gas or white-phosphorous grenades into thickets or holes in Viet Cong tunnels, forcing them out, retching, to be mowed down with machine gun fire. He wrote that the pilot spotted seven men in a rice paddy wearing black pyjamas: "The chopper whipped it with all guns blazing, killing three. The other four got away."

The article rather disgusted me, and I am sure that was intentional on my father's part. How did the helicopter crew know the men they killed were Viet Cong and not poor farmers? Indeed, no weapons were found on the three dead men. But anything that moved in the An Lao Valley was "considered fair game," Dad wrote, and the helicopters hunted with deadly efficiency. The body count was always in the Air Cav's favour, 30:1 on the day he flew with them, meaning thirty dead Viet Cong and one dead US soldier, a helicopter gunner. Lopsided body counts were "celebrated" as if they were sporting victories but they would not win the war, as the Americans would learn during the Tet Offensive in 1968, when gruesomely high NVA and Viet Cong body counts failed to deliver American overall victory even if the individual battles were tactical successes.

As I reviewed Dad's stories in the *Toronto Star* archives and the 1,000-word note he left me, I found no published reports about his time on the US aircraft carrier USS *Constellation,* even though I remember him talking about the thrill of reaching 250 kilometres per hour in two seconds as the steam catapult propelled his supply aircraft off the deck. Nor, surprisingly, was there a reference to what certainly was his most perilous mission: He went behind known North Vietnamese Army lines on a long-range reconnaissance patrol, or LRRP (pronounced "lurp"), with a small group of Marines. The LRRP soldiers were stealth fighters who sometimes had to engage in hand-to-hand combat in the Viet Cong tunnels into which they crawled, carrying nothing more than a pistol and a knife. Absolutely bonkers, I thought. Did he have a death wish?

This particular LRRP mission was to find NVA tunnels and mark them for air strikes. "The price to join the four-man lurp is to carry an M16 rifle and four fragmentation grenades," his note said. "A specially muffled Huey drops us. There is no smoking, no talking, just hand signals . . . One soldier strips and crawls inside [the tunnel]. Yep, this is the place. We slip back to an open spot, ignite an orange flare and, as the chopper comes in, we lace the shrubbery with gunfire, for a chopper is most vulnerable when it is descending. The big risk: a newsman armed is summarily shot if caught."

The use of "we" intrigued me. Was my father among the shooters? If so, he was firing not in defence, as he did in his foxhole next to the Ben Hai River in the DMZ at the start of his Vietnam trip, but in offence, which would put a new and highly troubling moral slant on his war reporting. I regret not having questioned him on the curious use of this pronoun while he was still kicking. I wanted to believe he did not shoot, even though he was armed as a condition of joining the patrol. But he may have.

The LRRP incident came late in his Vietnam trip. I wondered if his nerves were frazzled by then, if he was not thinking with the full clarity of a disinterested, professional journalist. It's possible that he was genuinely afraid and pulled the trigger instinctively, if he did pull it. It's also possible, on that particular minute of that particular day, moving in enemy territory, he considered the NVA the enemy. By then, he had spent close to three months in battle zones with the Americans, and American casualties would have bothered him more than Viet Cong or NVA casualties. Even though he considered the war tragic and morally repugnant, my father genuinely liked Americans, who he thought were more open and friendly than Canadians. Maybe he figured he was helping out comrades when he fired his rifle, if he fired his rifle. I will never know.

For all the drama of Dad's time in the field of combat, the newspaper stories that leave the deepest impression on me are these ones he wrote near the end of his Vietnam stay, in late July 1967, as the war was getting more intense by the day. They portrayed the "American war," as the Vietnamese call it, as a colossal mistake. At the time, my father's view was in the minority. Even as thousands of US troops were returning home in body bags—more than 58,000 of them died in the war—most Americans continued to buy the argument that Vietnam was a "domino" whose fall would enable communism to spread unchecked around the world.

In one article, Dad wrote that the Americans were making endless enemies through village "resettlement programs" such as the one he witnessed at Plei Beng: "The refugee population is swelling at an astounding rate all over Vietnam. It may also be creating more [Viet Cong]."

There was another article entitled "Vietnam Peasants Are the Losers in 'the Other War,'" which highlighted the cunning savagery that the Americans sometimes resorted to as the war of attrition gripped combatants on both sides with desperation and rage.

The Marines have an operation called "country fairs." They will surround a village before dawn, summon the inhabitants for some medical treatment, free teeth-pulling, music, candy for the kids—and propaganda. The Marines go into the village and exterminate those who have not joined the congregation, on the assumption those who stayed are VC.

In yet another article, he questioned Washington's optimism for victory, explaining that the American measure of success was the body count and the kill ratio, the (relatively small) number of US soldiers killed compared to the (relatively high) number of Viet Cong and NVA killed. These numbers are "recounted daily in the Saigon press briefings like football scores," he wrote, adding that the number of enemy troops allegedly killed was "sometimes preposterous." He also noted the "notorious reluctance" of the

South Vietnamese army to go into battle, the "endemic corruption" of the Saigon government, and the ever-more deadly weapons used by the NVA.

His conclusion: "The war can only be won by the Vietnamese; but it can be lost by the Americans."

It was not a popular conclusion when Dad came back to Chevy Chase in the summer of 1967, but one that time would justify. On April 30, 1975, a North Vietnamese T-54 tank smashed through the gates of the presidential palace in Saigon, ending the war and the fifteen-year US presence in Vietnam. By then, Dad was unhappily back in staid, dull Toronto after having covered the American war protests and race riots, the assassinations of Bobby Kennedy and Martin Luther King, the election of Richard Nixon in 1968, the Apollo moon shot, and, later, from his new *Toronto Star* base in Rome, the Biafran War, the Bangladesh Civil War and the Arab-Israeli conflicts in the Middle East. He had a sensational run. But no story riveted dad like Vietnam. To him, the war was the ultimate thrill, the ultimate reporting challenge. But he also saw it for what it was: the ultimate American travesty, and a tragedy for millions of Vietnamese. And he wrote that.

CHAPTER 13

My Mother's Agony

CHEVY CHASE, MARYLAND. *Spring-summer 1967*—In an era before the Internet or mobile phones, war correspondents had no way to contact their editors or families in a hurry. They could send telegrams if they could find a telegraph office, or pay off a hotel operator to move them up the waiting list for an overseas call over a crackling line. But once they were in the field, all communication was impossible. When Dad was in Vietnam, Mom had to track his whereabouts by reading his stories in the *Star*, which were delivered from Toronto once a week. Even the *Star's* foreign desk didn't know where he was until his stories landed. Regular phone calls from Edgar Ritchie, who was then Canada's ambassador to the United States, provided some comfort. Through his intelligence pipeline to Saigon, he could at least assure Mom that Dad was alive, or at least had been alive in the previous days. Today, foreign correspondents in danger zones, or potential danger zones, leave detailed itineraries with their editors, flight and hotel information, location and timing of interviews, contact information for interpreters, drivers and photographers, and arrange to send "all-safe" messages to the foreign desk at certain times of day. I'm sure my father found this no-leash reporting liberating; for my family, it was torture.

"I lost 30 pounds," Mom said, noting that she had been slim even before her husband went to Vietnam. "I am not exaggerating. I couldn't sleep. I got depressed. I knew he wasn't coming back."

My friend Kim remembered my mother falling apart:

> Bob's assignment would prove crushing to Ada. With three children to
> care for and no way of knowing whether her husband would return,
> Ada was a raw nerve. To the older children of the neighborhood, watch-
> ing her growing stress had a profound effect. Lizanne (Kim's older
> sister) decided never to marry a reporter or military man who could be
> stationed abroad. Ada internalized the stress, which then manifested
> itself as shingles, a painful skin condition. Summers in Washington
> were hot and humid and we had no air conditioners back then. Ada was
> reduced to pacing naked in her bedroom, as clothing was a maddening
> torture. Ada was in too much pain even to change a diaper . . . The eve-
> ning news was a relentless reminder of the danger of Bob's assignment.

My mother was saved by Valerie, Kim's mother. "Valerie looked after me,"
Mom said. "She asked me every day to come to supper." The meal was inevi-
tably preceded with a classic Chevy Chase relaxant: "She made a martini
for me, put two olives in it, and I just loved it. I had a drink every night."

Valerie was a churchgoing Catholic who got along well with the priest at
Our Lady of Lourdes Church in nearby Bethesda, Maryland. She charmed
the priest into asking the congregation to pray for Bob Reguly during
Sunday masses. For the first time in our corner of Chevy Chase, the war was
no longer an abstraction. On Woodside Place and the surrounding streets,
we weren't aware of any young men sent to Vietnam to fight, even though
the draft was in full swing—the sons of wealthy white men could always
find a way out. The American rock band Creedence Clearwater Revival
would later turn the theme of wealthy white exception into the chart-top-
ping song "Fortunate Son." It would become a countercultural anthem for
the tens of millions of teenagers and young adults who opposed the war.
But for now, prayers for Bob Reguly were the war's principal manifestation
in our neighbourhood, and they remained so until he arrived home in
July, 1967.

My father flew back through San Francisco and my mother met
him there for a romantic, welcome-home weekend. One of my favourite

pictures, which we mounted on a magnet that is still fastened to my fridge door in Rome, shows the two of them in front of the Balclutha steel-hulled sailing ship, built in 1886, that was turned into a museum and moored at Pier 41. My mother, wearing a knee-length white skirt, short white jacket, white gloves and high heels, looks like a movie star, with a hint of Jackie Kennedy about her. My father looks like a reporter out of Central Casting. He is leaner than he was before he left for Vietnam and wearing an allegedly bespoke silk suit that he bought during his layover in Hong Kong. It is laughably wrinkled. His smile is strained, perhaps because only a few days before the black and white photo was snapped, he was in a war zone.

When they returned to Chevy Chase, they were the toast of the town but my father wore out his welcome pretty fast. The ways in which Vietnam changed my father were plainly evident. He came back hating the war and hating US foreign policy. That contempt would stay with him for the rest of his life. He was convinced the Vietnam War was wrong, and that it was unwinnable in spite of US firepower. In spite of reassurances from LBJ and Secretary of Defense Robert McNamara that the war was just and being won. In spite of broad popular support for the war. In spite of the inconceivable notion that a country that had defeated Japan and Germany could be overpowered by a tiny nation of rice farmers.

My mother said, "He told me the Americans way overdid everything. They would come across a village and see someone working in the garden and they'd drop a bomb on them. How did they know they were Viet Cong? They didn't."

He told everyone what he had learned in Vietnam and it was a message that no one in our flag-waving, patriotic little neighbourhood wanted to hear, especially the Second World War and Korean War veterans. The concept of defeat was completely alien to them, obscene even, and they resented Dad for daring to suggest that it might all end badly for the mighty United States.

To be sure, Dad was on edge, maybe shell shocked, for a while. The time he reflexively punched me when I startled him from his sleep, or combat nightmare, told me as much. But he didn't have time to mope around the house, drowning himself in alcohol, nor was it his nature. The war protests and the civil rights movement were turning the streets into battle zones and he didn't want to miss another great show. So off he went again, this time wearing a cheap suit, not Army gear.

CHAPTER 14

Bobby Kennedy and a Breakdown

CHEVY CHASE, MARYLAND. 1967–1969—Not long after his return from Vietnam, Dad travelled more than ever, leaving the family for long periods of time to cover the vast canvas that was the United States. He covered civil rights marches, race riots, Vietnam War protests, the downfall of LBJ, the rise of Richard Nixon, and the Apollo rocket launches, including the Apollo 11 moon shot in 1969—he took the entire family with him to Cape Canaveral, Florida, to watch the lift-off. Famous people were always floating in and out of his life, and ours. I remember my father introducing me to the best-selling author Norman Mailer and Charles Lindbergh, the pilot who made the first non-stop solo flight across the Atlantic, who were both staying at our Florida hotel.

In July of 1967, right after he returned from Vietnam, he went to Harvard University to interview a young poet and novelist named Margaret Atwood, who was then twenty-seven and had just published *The Circle Game*, a collection of poems that won Canada's Governor General's Award for literary achievement. Atwood, with short brown curly hair, wearing a bright orange dress and flat shoes, was in fighting form. Ever the newsman, Dad concentrated on her political views, not her deft literary style, and extracted a fearsome pro-Canadian rant from her, noting her view, expressed in what he called a "taut, uncadenced voice that hints of suppressed excitement," that there was little time left to preserve "Canadianism" from the US economic and cultural onslaught. "We were wrong to let the bloody Yanks in," she said. "We've been sold to the USA and we ought to buy our country back piece by piece."

In March 1968, he wrote a five-part series on racism that would win him his third and final National Newspaper Award. I had pretty much forgotten about this award and only read the series, entitled "America's Other War," in 2020. I found it gripping. At a time when there was no Skype or Zoom for video calls, and before cheap and frequent flights became the norm, Dad did an astonishing number of interviews in five cities that either had been, or were about to be, torn apart by racial tension, protests, and violence. He presented a society that was effectively in the grip of apartheid. When I was reading the articles, I kept thinking: the details may have changed in the last half century, but not the themes.

In the section on Detroit, Dad presented a chilling view of a city not just divided along black-white lines, but preparing for war—an "arms race," as Dad called it. Paranoia and fear were replacing any hope of racial harmony. He wrote that the mayor of Dearborn, the white suburb on the edge of the city, was "an avowed segregationist [whose] call to arms is caused by the endemic fear of crazed Negroes invading from the Detroit Ghetto, something like the Barbarians sacking cultured Rome." He interviewed white housewives who, by the hundreds, were learning to use pistols to defend their homes, and separatist black Muslims who figured there was no hope for an integrated society and wanted to start the "Republic of New Afrika" in the US South.

In his Newark piece, he described the appalling poverty of the black slums. He wrote about the tiny bedroom of an apartment he visited, devoid of lightbulbs, where "the kids sleep like cord-wood," a rather Canadian reference to stacked firewood cut to uniform lengths.

The Philadelphia article was largely a profile of Frank Rizzo, the city's notoriously racist police chief, and later mayor, who was known as "the father of the police state." Rizzo was so intent on building a military-style force to put down black protestors that he even armed his firefighters (his statue would be vandalized, and later removed, from downtown Philadelphia during the Black Lives Matter protests in 2020).

Dad's Chicago piece proved remarkably prescient. He wrote about the possibility of the Yippie countercultural movement inspired by Abbie Hoffman and Jerry Rubin coalescing with the anti-war movement, turning the city into a battle zone. That is exactly what happened a few months later, during the Democratic National Convention of 1968. Dad was there to report on it and my mother and I spotted him on TV, the Nikkormat camera he had carried through Vietnam slung over his chest.

In some ways, 1968 was the most exciting year of my father's career. America was on the edge of revolution, my mother remembers Dad telling her, and he had a front-row seat to it all. At age ten, I was too young to understand the forces at play, but I do have one vivid memory. Washington DC exploded in rage and violence after the assassination of black civil rights leader Martin Luther King Jr. in Memphis, Tennessee, on April 4, 1968. From Chevy Chase, we could see the smoke from the burning streets a few kilometres away and our TV screens were filled with images of thousands of heavily armed soldiers sent into the capital by LBJ to restore order. One morning, just before Dad headed to King's hometown of Atlanta to report on the aftermath of the assassination, I begged him to drive me into Washington to see the destruction. He did, sort of. We got pretty close, but did not actually enter the burnt-out areas. Then he dropped me back into the safety of Chevy Chase and sped back downtown. It was his way of planting the journalistic seed in me.

Other than Vietnam, the event that shook him most deeply in those years was the assassination of Bobby Kennedy during the 1968 election campaign.

Some of America's biggest cities were still no-go zones in June of that year. King's assassination two months earlier had triggered a wave of rioting and protests against social inequality. At the same time, mass protests against the Vietnam War were filling the streets and shutting down universities across the United States and in Europe. Draft board offices were attacked by anti-war protestors and set ablaze. The moment seemed ripe for Robert F. Kennedy, younger brother of the assassinated president, JFK. He was fighting a close race with Hubert Humphrey for the Democratic Party's presidential nomination. Humphrey had become a vigorous opponent of the war. Kennedy, who was especially popular with young voters, was also opposed to the war and was promoting a peace plan to end the bombing of North Vietnam, withdraw US and North Vietnamese troops from South Vietnam, and replace them with international troops. When Kennedy launched his run for the nomination in March 1968, he openly said the war was unwinnable: "our present course will not bring victory, will not bring peace, will not stop the bloodshed. . . ."

Kennedy became the Democratic front-runner after winning the crucial California primary on June 4, 1968. Shortly after midnight, he was in the ballroom of the Ambassador Hotel in Los Angeles as his supporters cheered him on. My father scuttled backstage to wait for Kennedy, who was to meet the press. Kennedy entered a door from the stage that led to the hotel's kitchen and shook hands with a few of the kitchen employees. At that point, Dad was one of about fifteen people in the room. He was standing not nine metres from Kennedy when Sirhan Sirhan's shots rang out, hitting the New York senator in the back of the head with .22 calibre bullets from near point-blank range. My father watched as several men, including Rosey Grier, the beefy former professional footballer who was Kennedy's bodyguard, wrestled Sirhan to the ground and grabbed his pistol.

Dad's account of the assassination appeared in the June 5 editions of the *Toronto Star* under the enormous headline: "Surgeon fears extensive brain damage, Bobby 'May Never Recover.'" Underneath the headline was a photo of Kennedy on the floor, bleeding; a rosary had been placed in his hand by a kitchen busboy. Here are the opening paragraphs of his piece, one of the few times Dad wrote in the first person:

LOS ANGELES—I was standing about 30 feet away from Senator Robert Kennedy when he was shot earlier today.

The shots sounded more like Chinese firecrackers popping than the sharp crack of gunfire.

There was a stunned silence, then screams and pandemonium.

A giant Negro, football star Rosey Grier, was trying to wrestle a snub-nosed revolver out of the hands of a swarthy, skinny young man in rumpled denims.

"I did it for the good of my country," the man was saying, sort of moaning the words.

I pushed past as three more men began pummelling the gunman and saw Kennedy lying on his back, clutching his left abdomen.

Blood seemed to be coming from his right ear, but it was hard to tell as the dark pool formed under his head. Kennedy opened his eyes. He was alive.

Kennedy's last words a few minutes later were "Don't lift me" as he was being hoisted onto a stretcher. He died twenty-six hours later, in the early hours of June 6, at the Good Samaritan Hospital. My father had not slept for a minute in the interval and had pumped out a remarkably detailed piece about Sirhan's Palestinian upbringing and the Israeli occupation that may have motivated his desire to kill Kennedy, who Sirhan considered pro-Israeli. The article, astonishing in its detail and depth, and the speed with which he put it together, carried the headline: "How a miserable refugee camp gave birth to an assassin."

The next day, after reporting and writing furiously for more than two days, Dad went to a bar in Los Angeles and broke down in tears, the only time an assignment ripped him apart emotionally and visibly for all to see. He told me that he believed that Kennedy was the only candidate who would stop the war and that his death was a great loss for America. "What a waste it was," he told me decades after he covered the assassination.

I am still trying to understand this bar-room breakdown. In Vietnam the year before, he had seen dozens, maybe hundreds of corpses, mutilated in the most horrific ways. He had seen dead children and wounded American soldiers screaming in agony. He had seen a US Marine take a bullet between the eyes in a vicious battle in the DMZ, the swath of no-man's land that separated North and South Vietnam. Yet none of that carnage seemed to affect him as did Kennedy's death. I suspect that Dad had built up an emotional attachment to Kennedy, who he saw as a moral man, and had let his normally disinterested approach to reporting slip. My father, too, had concluded when he was in Vietnam that the war was unwinnable and that the Americans had to find a way out that did not smell of outright defeat.

I remember him returning from Los Angeles looking exhausted, hollowed out, even. Then my mother packed his bags and he was off again: there was an election, and race riots, and Vietnam War protests, and the moon shot to cover.

I was old enough to remember his absences during our Washington years. He rarely played with us kids, never changed a diaper, never cooked a meal, never cleaned the house. He would buy me what I now consider "guilt" presents, like the little gasoline-powered fly-by-wire airplane—I inherited his love for flying machines—that he helped me send aloft precisely once before losing interest. I thought it was perfectly normal for fathers to disappear for days or weeks at a time, only to come home exhausted, sleep for two days, and hit the bottle. At least his journeys weren't dangerous, most of the time.

Decades later, when I was running from one assignment to another in Europe, the Middle East, and North Africa, covering everything from terrorist attacks and political assassinations to elections and climate conferences, I would understand that foreign corresponding was often a non-stop roller-coaster, with little time for rest or reflection, all the more so since digital journalism meant I would never actually be off deadline. The newspaper journalists from Dad's era faced one or two print deadlines a day.

CHAPTER 15

Wars Without End
and A Kidnapping

ROME, THE MIDDLE EAST, *Africa, Bangladesh. 1969–1972—* When Robert Reguly died in February of 2011, tributes and condolences from dozens of his friends and colleagues poured into my email inbox. The one from Don North, a former Vietnam War correspondent who worked with my father when he launched his TV career after quitting the *Toronto Star* in 1973, captured Dad's reporting style perfectly:

> He saw himself as one of the guardians of the peoples' right to know. He was from a special kind of journalism, the "if your mother says she loves you, check it out" school of journalism. His credo: Afflict the comfortable and comfort the afflicted. Bob gave himself a license to seek the truth, reminding us now that the most important credential is a conscience that cannot be purchased or silenced.

As I read and reread my father's articles after his death, especially those from his post-Vietnam years, I realized that North was right. My father was a thrill seeker, to be sure, but this was not what drove his journalistic agenda. If he went to danger spots, it was because he was courageous and wanted to see for himself what was happening on the ground, not because he was an action junkie who needed to get his kicks. His aphrodisiac was not so much living life on the edge as exposing the truth about tragedy or corruption, not necessarily in war zones. In his later years as a newspaper reporter, and as a reporter for a high-profile Canadian investigative weekly TV news show, *W5*, he covered topics as varied as environmental damage by corporations, harassment by the Church of Scientology, the health dangers of cheap cosmetics, Canada's woefully inadequate military hardware, sleazy politicians, and politicians blackmailed by the Soviets in the Cold War. These confirmed his reputation as a hard-hitting, take-no-prisoners reporter. I remember him using the term "champions of the overdog" to describe most of the mainstream Canadian and American media during his era, including my own employer, *The Globe and Mail,* which he considered a bit too cozy with the Canadian business establishment, and the rival *National Post,* which he considered the undiluted voice of the establishment. His era of journalism was one that abhorred first-person reporting, a time when newspapers were seen as bastions of integrity and impartiality whose goal was to build trust among broad swathes of readers, not narrow interest groups with political agendas. The term "fake news" did not exist until the advent of online media. Fox News-style partisan ranting did not exist until TV cable channels gave themselves licence to abandon disinterested reporting and take sides.

My father's goal, and the goal of his colleagues in the 1950s, 1960s, and 1970s was simply to report what was really happening, and to find out what politicians and businessmen were trying to hide. Dad considered his job as a reporter a glorious opportunity to attack the devil, as the renowned nineteenth-century British newspaperman, William Stead, an investigative journalism pioneer, put it. My father just did it better than a lot of his colleagues and rivals. "He was a hero to all us young future reporters in the 1960s and 1970s—our own [Bob] Woodward and [Carl] Bernstein," Roy MacGregor, the Canadian author and former columnist and feature writer at *The Globe and Mail,* said in the paper's full-page obituary in February of 2011, comparing my father to the American journalists whose investigation into the Watergate scandal in the early 1970s brought down President

Richard Nixon. Ted Gorsline, a great friend of my father who worked with Dad at the Ontario government during his post-journalism years, told me that thrills were never Dad's main career motivation. "He was the finest, bravest, and most honourable man I ever met," Gorsline told me long after Dad's death. "He was a stand-alone. The most important thing to Bob was his honour. He never dealt it away. Not ever. It was more important to him than his family." My family learned that truth the hard way. When Dad was working in communications for Province of Ontario in the mid-1980s after his staff reporting career came to a crashing end, he suffered a heart attack and had to pull back from full employment. The government offered him a full pension that would have made my parents' retirement years exceedingly comfortable. Incredibly, Dad turned down the offer because he felt he didn't deserve it—he had worked for the government for only a few years. The decision mystified and enraged my mother, Ada, who by then was suffering from terrible back pain and was eager to quit work at a local optical shop to help pay the bills. But Gorsline got it. "I think to him the full pension looked like a payoff," Gorsline told me. "I would have taken it. He destroyed himself and his family for his honour."

In my journey to understand my father, I have come to see that what made him a superb journalist was his quest—not for adventure, but to expose lies and misinformation. Dad became a war correspondent by accident, really. He never made it his life ambition to cover wars. If he had not won a National Newspaper Award for the Gerda Munsinger scoop, he would not have been sent to the Washington DC bureau. If he were not in Washington, he would not gone to Vietnam. Yes, he loved the action and danger of war, but he did so not because he treated his life as a non-stop roller-coaster ride; he did it mostly because he wanted to write what was really happening. His Vietnam pieces were not just descriptions of combat scenes, soaked in blood. A few were, of course, but many were anti-war portraits of misery or analytical pieces that left the reader thinking: What a brutal, unjust, unnecessary—and futile—war this was. The war filled him with great sadness—and hatred for American foreign policy—and he conveyed this in his dispatches. "Your father was a hero to my generation of reporters because he had a big heart as well as a nose for a good story,"

Susan Reisler, a former Canadian Broadcasting Corp. reporter told me after Dad's death.

Vietnam would be one of four conflicts that my father would cover as he made his transformation from Canadian investigative reporter in his early and mid-thirties to globetrotting foreign correspondent in his late thirties and into his forties. He enjoyed the new routine, even if came at some expense to his profile—he would never again be as famous as he was during his Hal Banks and Gerda Munsinger years. He was maturing as a journalist and as a man. He wanted to know how the world worked, and write about it in a scrupulous and fair-minded way. His canvas was expanding, even if, late in his journalistic career, he would return to investigative reporting exclusively in Canada.

Dad's three years in Washington taught him that Canada did not much matter on the world stage and that its problems, while ample when viewed from Toronto, Montreal, or the middle of the Prairies, were relatively trivial compared to the miseries suffered in the poor Black areas of Detroit and Newark, or in the no-hope towns of the Deep South, whose gullible sons were swept off the streets by the draft and dumped in the killing fields of Vietnam. His next three years, when Europe, the Middle East, Africa, and much of Asia were his stomping grounds, taught him that even the United States' problems, by global standards, were nothing compared to the depth of suffering and misery he saw in Biafra, Gaza, East Pakistan (now Bangladesh), and elsewhere.

I had always been aware of Dad's experiences around the world, and they became more real to me as I followed in his footsteps as a foreign correspondent for *The Globe and Mail*. It was only in the summer of 2020, when the COVID-19 pandemic all but ended my ability to travel, that I had the time to try to understand his motivations. I hunkered down in a friend's ancient farmhouse in Umbria, in central Italy, and read every story I could find—hundreds of them—that Dad wrote from mid-1969 to late 1972, when Rome was his base. I found most, but not all, in the *Toronto Star* archives that now languish in the databases of the Toronto Public Library. Those stories, plus the few typed notes he left me at my request shortly before he died, and some photos he took that are held by the library, allowed me to piece together his assignments from some of the world's most dangerous hotspots. The effort was rewarding but not easy. The articles survive in the form of grainy PDFs, legible only with the help of a magnifying glass. At the end of each day, I went to bed with a headache due to eye strain and—also likely—the emotional tension caused by the images of death, war and famine, and the realization of quite how much misery, cruelty, desperation, and heartache Dad witnessed.

There are too many stories, too many destinations, too many themes, to sum up Dad's overseas stint in one tight nugget. But a few things stand out. The main one was his ability to get off the beaten track to find the story behind the story. Very little of his reporting used quotes from official government, military, or corporate PRs. Honing the skills he learned in Vietnam, he avoided the party line and went directly to the primary source, typically the actual war zone or the scene of the crime or atrocity. He had no interest in reporting the bullshit body-count figures spewed out by any general or commander bent on declaring a victory where none existed.

This tactic is evident in Dad's reporting of the Nigerian Civil War, which started in 1967 and ended three years later, after some two million civilians starved to death. Dad was in Nigeria's biggest city, Lagos, when the war was winding down in late 1969 and early 1970. The government spokesmen (they were all men) were telling reporters that no one was starving in Biafra, the oil-rich but impoverished breakaway southern state that was fighting the Nigerian government. The government claimed that ample food supplies were en route and that there was no need for foreign aid. Seasoned by his years in Vietnam, Dad knew he needed to verify the official line; he cut short his visit to Lagos and headed to Biafra to find out what was happening for himself. What he saw, and photographed, was shocking.

In Owerri, the last of the three capitals of the short-lived Republic of Biafra, he opened his story, published on January 23, with a first-hand account that left no doubt of a Biafran starvation crisis. Under the headline "Star Man Sees Refugees Trampled Fighting for Flour," he wrote:

> The army truck roared into the wretched refugee camp and three sol-
> diers threw two sacks of flour at the 2,000 huddled Igbos [the largely

Christian ethnic group that dominated Biafra]. Two were trampled to death in the ensuing scramble . . . Undeniably, many children are slowly starving.

At that time, articles could be transmitted faster than photos; the raw film had to be flown to the photo editors a continent away if a wire transmitter could not be found. So, his gruesome photographic evidence arrived three days later. The full-page spread featured four of his photos, their tragic images indelible. They showed internally displaced Igbos who had emerged from the forest, where they had fled when the bullets began flying, looking like victims in a concentration camp. In one photo, a young, emaciated woman, her eyes haunted, stretches out her hand for food. In another, a tiny Biafran boy squats in the dirt, crying as he looks at the camera and the photographer—my father. The naked boy's belly is distended with disease, his arms and legs thin as sticks. He is alone, an orphan. In the background, slightly out of focus, a group of children, equally malnourished, look the other way. I think it was my father's most powerful published photo.

Years later, my father told me that the child almost certainly died shortly after the photo was taken. How he photographed such misery with the sort of professional detachment that allowed him to walk away, file the story, and move on to the next story without having a breakdown, day after day, horror after horror, is beyond me. I can only imagine that the brain wiring that muted his fear response also muted his immediate emotional response. This is not to say he was heartless, quite the opposite—he was exceedingly generous in spirit. I think the nature of his job demanded, or ensured, that his emotional walls rose the moment he was on assignment. I doubt I could have shown the same fortitude. As a journalist, I am not convinced I could have simply walked away from the sight of the dead and they dying and leapt into the next story without missing a beat. Dad and I were similar in many ways. We both loved exciting, even dangerous, assignments, both felt empathy for the oppressed, both took our careers exceedingly seriously, to the point we were absentee fathers a lot of the time. But we were different in many ways, too. While my father thought expressing emotion was unmanly, a sign of weakness even, I always wore my heart on my sleeve and could get quite emotional at times, as I did during my week covering the aftermath of the 9/11 terrorist attacks in Manhattan in 2001. The Catholic priest who married Karen and me in 1994 in Manhattan, Mychal Judge, was the chaplain for the New York City Fire Department. He was the first certified fatality in the attacks at the World Trade Center and I went to his funeral four days after the towers fell. I cried on and off for more than a week, to the point I could not sleep and had trouble making deadline on some days for what was one of the biggest stories of my career. I cannot imagine my father breaking down like I did. Weeping at his desk would have been socially taboo in the testosterone-charged newsrooms of that era. Could I have taken a photo of a dying Biafran child and walk away an instant later? I don't know; maybe not.

A test of Dad's professional integrity came early in his Rome stint, in 1970, after he had made several swings though the Middle East. At the time, the Arab world was united in its opposition to Israel, which, in a series of lightning fast and brilliant tactical moves in the Six-Day War in June 1967, had seized the Gaza Strip, the Sinai Peninsula from Egypt, the West Bank and East Jerusalem from Jordan, and the Golan Heights from Syria. My father was covering the Middle East when both sides were preparing for another all-out, map-reshaping conflict and the Palestinian Liberation Organization was fighting a war of attrition with Israel. Murders, kidnappings, bombings, and guerrilla attacks were almost daily events during the late 1960s and early 1970s, leading up to the Yom Kippur War in October 1973.

A typical trip would see him visit Cairo, Amman, Damascus, Beirut, Cyprus, and Tel Aviv, usually in that order, using two Canadian passports, one of which would not show Israeli entry stamps because any evidence of having visited Israel would have excluded his entry into the Arab countries. Dad was adept at identifying military hardware and, as a journalist, had some access to military bases in the Arab countries, as long as an official minder was present. At a southern Egyptian air base, he noticed a fleet of supersonic, long-range, Soviet-built MiG-19 interceptors. He knew they were long range because they had moulded, integral belly tanks, instead of the standard, under-wing drop tanks. Suddenly, the planes were scrambled and six pilots ran to the cockpits of six MiG aircraft. "Ground crews trundled out a single gasoline-powered generator, plugged in one plane at a time. It took half an hour to launch six planes," my father said in a note he wrote a few months before he died.

Back in Rome, he met an American friend who lived nearby, and told him about the ridiculously long time it took the Egyptians to launch their fighter jets, leaving them exposed on the ground to Israeli attack. Dad knew Joe (not his real name) was a CIA man, even though he would never admit to it. I remember hanging out with Joe's daughters, who assumed their father had some bland job at the US embassy. Joe was impressed. "How about this?" he asked my father. "When you return from a trip, we'll just have lunch with one of our Middle East experts and we'll pay you a retainer."

Dad demurred. By then, he knew US intelligence services were notoriously leaky and that if word got out in the Arab countries that he was on the CIA payroll, he would face execution as an American spy. "'No thanks', I told him," Dad wrote in the notes he left me. "'Let's pretend this conversation never happened and we can still be friends.'"

In fact, Dad was mistaken for an Israeli spy not long after, and his penchant to get up close and personal almost cost him his life. He was on assignment in southern Lebanon in August 1970, when the Israeli-Palestinian conflict was in full swing. He was touring the enormous Ain al-Hilweh Palestinian refugee camp the day after Israeli F-4 Phantom jets bombed it, claiming it was a recruiting centre for terrorists. His escorts were two members of the Popular Front for the Liberation of Palestine (PFLP), the famously effective group of Christian fighters who invented passenger-jet hijackings and who, a month later, would blow up three empty hijacked passenger jets at the Dawson's Field desert airstrip in Jordan. As they were viewing the destruction of the refugee camp, two men carrying AK-47 assault rifles kidnapped Dad and his escorts. They were taken into a nearby building. He was ordered to sit on a wooden kitchen chair while a sheikh in white robes shouted at him and the PFLP men. "While the two kidnappers waved their guns, another man turned his kitchen chair to face me, knee-to-knee, pulled out a Browning 9-mm pistol and held it against my belly, the hammer cocked," my father's notes read—he wrote about the episode in the *Toronto Star*. "My rule was never to show fear." He knew it could be mistaken for guilt.

After an hour of high tension and yelling in Arabic, his PFLP escorts convinced the sheikh that Dad really was a reporter and they were all freed. My father learned from his escorts that he could have been killed at any moment. The kidnappers and the sheikh were on edge because they had captured an Israeli Mossad agent posing as a Canadian reporter a few days earlier. He confessed under torture, probably by being skinned alive, and was killed.

In another incident, back in Canada, Dad learned from the RCMP that French Barbouzes hitmen were planning to kill him for a 1978 newspaper article that exposed the presence of a dozen of them who had relocated to Montreal. The Barbouzes were notoriously savage French undercover agents. They had merrily garrotted their way through the Algerian War, waging a terror campaign against the Organisation Armée Secrète, the French paramilitary organization trying to prevent Algerian independence. "They'll try to make it look like an accident," the RCMP officer, Moe Goguen, told Dad, according to his notes to me. Dad played it cool. He gambled correctly that the Barbouzes would not risk whacking a high-profile journalist for fear of retaliation by the police.

My father's assignments in the Middle East, Africa, and Asia still fill me with awe. The risks he took to get stories were, in my view, on par with the risks he took in Vietnam a few years earlier. How he survived the Bangladesh Liberation War in 1971, when East Pakistan (now Bangladesh) won independence from Pakistan, astounds me. He told me the sheer inhumanity he saw in East Pakistan in 1970 and 1971 made the Vietnam War look benign. The opening paragraph of a story he wrote from Dacca, now the capital of Bangladesh, in September 1971, read: "The butchery continues in East Pakistan, the green land splotched with the blood of perhaps a 100 My Lais."

He was referring to the My Lai massacre in South Vietnam in March 1968, when American troops murdered as many as 500 unarmed Vietnamese civilians, including babies— a horrific incident that was exposed by US investigative reporter Seymour Hersh a year and a half later and triggered revulsion around the world. In East Pakistan, my father wrote about the mind-numbing savagery of both sides of the war. One incident involved Bengali guerrillas, who were setting up an ambush for Pakistani government troops:

> In Paksey [in east-central Bangladesh], guerrillas use crucified girls as army ambush bait. They nail the girls to a crude crucifix beside the road and soak them in gasoline. At the sound of an army jeep patrol's approach, the girl is set alight. The soldiers usually stop at the grisly sight—and make fine targets.

Dad and I did not talk much about the war in Bangladesh—most of our war chat centred on Vietnam—but a few grisly anecdotes stand out. He told me that he was once in a small, sampan-style boat paddled by a guide along a river tributary. He dropped his camera overboard while taking a shot, dove in to retrieve it and almost got tangled in the mass of bodies all roped together at the bottom. In another, he and some soldiers—I cannot remember which side they were on—entered a village. They swung open a wooden door, under which they had spotted a pool of blood. Several babies were dangling from the inside of the door, spikes driven through their heads.

Not all his experiences were blood curdling. One of his stories is rip-roaring sensational, like a scene from a Hollywood adventure movie. He and a photographer, whose name I cannot remember, were in a Bengali village in a river delta. A small Pakistani patrol boat arrived unexpectedly and discharged a few troops carrying automatic rifles. Dad and his friend realized they all risked getting slaughtered. Their escape plan was audacious, but, against all odds, it worked. They quickly paid a couple of dozen peasants to storm the boat. They tossed the one or two soldiers guarding the boat overboard, fired up the engine, and sped off. Dad said the photographer he was with would get killed on assignment a year or so later, in southeast Asia—it was a time when photographers were getting kidnapped and executed with alarming regularity.

But the overseas stories of his that made the greatest impression on me were not the ones of atrocities in Bangladesh or starving children in Biafra.

What impressed me the most was the four-part series he wrote in 1971 after visiting Palestinian refugee camps in southern Lebanon, Gaza, Ramallah (the main Palestinian city in the West Bank, then part of Occupied Jordan) and the Sinai Peninsula. The Western media did not report much on the plight of Palestinian refugees, who had fled or had been expelled from their country during the 1947–49 Palestinian War (known in Israel as the War of Independence) and the Six-Day War of 1967. They were already a forgotten people, as they are in the twenty-first century, not visited often by the foreign correspondents, who were usually based in Israel.

Dad delved into the refugee camps and presented their hardships and despair in vivid, unvarnished reporting. In the Ramallah camp, he interviewed Aref al-Aref, a renowned Arab historian who had been mayor of East Jerusalem in the 1950s and was then aged seventy-seven. "The crimes of our occupants," Aref told him, "have no parallel since the Middle Ages."

He wrote about Israelis removing textbooks from Palestinian schools, of the Israeli policy of "collective punishment," and the general lack of freedom, sanitation, decent housing, jobs, and access to medical and dental care in the camps. Gaza then was full of malnourished children and remains one of the biggest "food insecure" spots on the planet, according to the United Nations World Food Programme. "They die like flies," an English nurse, Jan Smit, told my father.

The series earned lavish praise from the Canadian Arab community and universal condemnation from Israeli and Jewish groups. The Canadian Arab Federation cited my father's "courageous reporting." Another Arab reader in Canada called him "an honest and fearless observer who is not out to please anybody except those who wish to know the truth." Aba Gefen, who was then the Israeli Consul General in Toronto, dismissed my father as a terrorist sympathizer. "Only those who support Arab terrorism repeat the lies about atrocities and Mr. Reguly does not hide his feelings," he wrote in a lengthy letter to the editor in August 1971.

Just as my father went to Vietnam thinking the United States would win the war, only to conclude the opposite within a few weeks of watching the North Vietnamese and American soldiers kill one another, his views on the Middle East would undergo a similar transformation. Before he visited the Middle East, he was pro-Israeli. By 1970, after he had made a few trips to region, including the Palestinian refugee camps, his sympathy for Israel had vanished, even though he enjoyed visiting the country and had many Israeli friends and contacts, one of whom had helped him with the Gerda Munsinger scoop in 1966.

Dad's Middle East reporting won him no friends in the Canadian Jewish community who, according to my father, put enormous pressure on his editors to direct him away from writing about the Israeli-Palestinian conflict. I do know from trawling through his stories that, by mid-1971, his trips to the Middle East became rarer, possibly because his editors encouraged him to go elsewhere. Dad believed that one of the reasons he was yanked from Rome after little more than three years was because his editors were getting worn down by complaints from the Israeli lobby about his coverage. I will never know for sure, though Dad was miserable when he found himself back in the newsroom in Toronto in the autumn of 1972. His uncharacteristically dark mood was no doubt intensified by the death of his mother. Within a year, he would quit the paper and go into TV journalism. Ted Gorsline told me the final straw was the *Toronto Star*'s refusal to print the results of an investigation he had done on Alan Eagleson, the high-profile lawyer, National Hockey League agent, and former Ontario politician who was considered the top hockey promoter in the sport. It turned out that Dad was years ahead of his time on the Eagleson scandal. In the mid-1990s, Eagleson was charged in the United States and Canada with defrauding his hockey clients and skimming money from tournaments, thrown into prison and disbarred.

Dad's spectacular career at the *Toronto Star* had ended on a down note.

I, too, was miserable when we returned to Toronto in late 1972, where I was relegated to the cold, low-ceilinged basement of our tiny 1930s house in the Beaches neighbourhood of Toronto. In Rome, we had lived like princes and princesses: we had a big, luxurious apartment in a compound with a pool—two, actually—endless sunshine, enrolment in international schools, exotic holidays, a cleaning lady, a cute little Fiat 850 car as well as the monster Ford Falcon Dad had bought in Chevy Chase. I did not just miss the material benefits of life in Rome, I also missed the friends and fascinating drop-in guests—the diplomats, spies, reporters, politicians, and academics. In Rome, as I entered my teen years, I was old enough to revel in my father's career, and began yearning to be like him. By the time I was thirteen I was begging him to take me on reporting assignments so I could see him in action. He refused to take me to the Middle East, because he was convinced another war was coming—the Yom Kippur War would rip the Middle East apart again a year after we left Rome—but he brought me along on a couple of tamer assignments. One was to cover an earthquake near Ancona, a seaport city on Italy's Adriatic coast, where the only hotel we could find that was still open shook all night from aftershocks, terrifying me, but not Dad—he just rolled over and went back to sleep.

In June 1971, I convinced Dad to take me to Malta to cover the election of Dom Mintoff, the socialist and nationalist leader of the country's Labour Party who was determined to severe the last colonial ties with the United Kingdom. We arrived in Valletta, Malta's capital, on a BOAC flight from Rome and jumped into a taxi. Valletta was in chaos, with throngs of chanting crowds waving flags and setting off fireworks. There was smoke everywhere. As we pulled up to the elegant old Hotel Phoenicia, an Art Deco pile built in the 1930s just beyond Valletta's historic centre, we saw a column of smoke that seemed to come from within the hotel, whose entrance was blocked by the police. Whether the smoke was from an accidental fire or a bomb we did not know. "I guess we have to find another hotel," my father said, calmly, as if burning hotels were a minor annoyance. We kept driving until we found a new place. Sitting in the back seat of the taxi, snapping photos out the window with Dad's Nikkormat, I was thrilled.

The next day, I was in Mintoff's office—he arrived late—with Dad and a few other foreign reporters. I remember the BBC correspondent in a wrinkled, light grey suit, sweating away, looking at his watch every minute, no doubt wondering how he would make deadline. Mintoff was surprisingly short and wearing his trademark thick, black-framed glasses. He did not seem to mind the lanky North American teenager with a camera and gave me a smile before firing off answers as the reporters flung questions at him. When he was finished, the reporters charged off. Dad and I galloped back to our hotel and I heard him banging away on his portable typewriter, the same one he used in Vietnam—the little white and grey Olympus that now sits in my office in Rome. After deadline, we went for a late dinner in the crazy streets of Valletta, which were full of chanting voters, placards, flags, and revelry. I was in heaven, tingling with excitement on that fevered hot night. I too wanted to be a foreign correspondent.

A Broken Man, A Proud Son

T*ORONTO. 2011*—The last time I saw my father was in early January 2011. He was a week or two short of his eightieth birth-day, bedridden in Toronto's Sunnybrook Hospital. I had flown in from Rome and my mother, Ada, was with me. Dad had lost an enormous amount of weight and was barely eating.

Even though he was fading, his mind was intact and he could talk lucidly in short bursts before tiring out. He had not been able to shave, or get shaved, in a week or two and he looked like an old bear. I lathered up his face and shaved him, slowly, being careful not to cut the skin. Doing so broke my heart. My father, my superman, was helpless, and we knew that for all his outward bravado and upbeat spirits, he was terrified of death.

But what a fighter. In the late summer, thanks to the urging of my ever stalwart and attentive sisters, Susan and Rebecca, he received a mechanical heart valve, a risky operation that the doctors warned could kill him, given his age and heart disease. He survived the ordeal and was recovering in the autumn. I saw him not long after the surgery, when he was back in his Toronto home, on his feet and chipper. I figured he had bought himself a few more years. But his old macho attitude caught up him. Later in the autumn he suffered from a relentless nose bleed, lost a lot of blood and refused to go to the hospital before it was too late. From then on, it was all downhill. Trips to the hospital by ambulance became distressingly regular. He was sent home to die in late January, although I still believed he would linger for months, or longer, since he had surprised us so many times by emerging from near-death experiences. It was force of will, and robust peasant genes. My mother and my sisters were by his side when he finally let go on February 24, 2011. I was back in Italy. They said his last days were horrendous and they are still scarred from watching him suffer. His morphine injections came too late to ease him painlessly into the next world.

In truth, most of my father's final three decades were joyless and often painful, emotionally, psychologically, and physically. His professional downfall was swift and merciless and it certainly accelerated his health problems.

When Dad quit the *Toronto Star* in 1973, a year after our return from Rome, his career was still flying high. He made the uneasy transition to TV at Canada's CTV national television network, where he worked at the *W5* weekly investigative programme and at CTV Reports, the network's documentary unit. One of his hour-long documentaries, on toxic cosmetics, won gold at a documentary festival in New York. Other pieces explored pollution by Canadian industrial companies, and the police surveillance of a remote camp in northwestern Ontario that was associated with Jim Jones, the American cult leader and self-professed faith healer who coerced the mass suicide and murder of 918 of his followers in Jonestown, Guyana in 1978.

While Dad's TV career was a success, he found TV exhausting and frustrating—he compared it to "carrying a 10-ton pencil." He yearned to get back into print where he could be independent and move fast, without a team. In his newspaper career, he had always been a one-man show.

He got his wish, landing at the *Toronto Sun*, the upstart tabloid that grew out of the ashes of the *Toronto Telegram* in 1971. He worked for four years as its senior investigative correspondent, producing some remarkable original articles, although nothing on the scale of his Hal Banks or Gerda Munsinger scoops.

His downfall came in June 1981, just as I was starting my master's degree in journalism at the University of Western Ontario, his alma mater. He was involved in a scoop that backfired spectacularly. The *Sun* had hired a hotshot former hockey reporter named Donald Ramsay, who was twenty-eight years old and working on a sensational story. A senior federal cabinet minister, John Munro, was said to be profiting from the insider trading of shares of Petrofina Canada before it was bought by Petro-Canada, the national oil company. Ramsay claimed he had microfiche of foreign bank accounts that proved Munro's Petrofina share ownership.

My father was called in late in the game to support Ramsay's reporting but grew wary and recommended that the story be held the day before it was to be published. But Ramsay pushed back. He somehow convinced his editors and Dad that his research was sound and the piece went to print with my father's byline running in second spot. Munro claimed the story was an outright falsehood, sued for libel, and won, a closed case after Ramsay could not produce the microfiche he had said he possessed. Ramsay was fired. Dad resigned. "I think I'm finished in the newspaper business," he told the Canadian Press news agency on June 12, 1981. "There's an informal network at newspapers. Once you're tarred with this, how could I write a bylined story on politics without getting laughed at?"

I met Ramsay a couple of times when Dad would invite him home for dinner. His erratic, frenetic behaviour troubled me. My mother said she felt the same. He vanished after the Munro fiasco and later surfaced as a media relations man for the Winnipeg Jets of the National Hockey League. He died of liver failure in 1994 in Vancouver. Decades after the incident, my mother and I still wonder why Robert Reguly, one of Canada's most seasoned investigative journalists, trusted a young, inexperienced reporter and attached his byline to the piece when he had doubts about its accuracy.

During the libel trial in 1982, my father admitted he had not seen the microfiche that Ramsay claimed was in his possession and that allegedly proved Munro was a crook. My mother said that Dad had asked to see it, triggering an incensed reaction from Ramsay. "Ramsay kept telling him, 'I've got the microfiche. Don't you trust me? Do you think I'm a liar?'" she told me. "Bob said he believed the guy. 'Why would he lie to me? He had been working on the story for four months.'"

In his twenty-seven years as a front-line journalist, my father was never once accused of fabricating a story, or even a quote. Like any good investigative reporter, he did attract libel notices from people who tried to use legal intimidation to stop his pursuit, but all of them were withdrawn or dismissed. He was a meticulous researcher and he always worked alone. Making my way through the *Toronto Star* archives, I did not spot a single double-bylined article.

The truth was that for all his cynicism and skepticism, he trusted his friends and colleagues, never imagining that they could or would act dishonourably. He considered Ramsay a friend as well as a colleague. His trust was a tragic, career-busting mistake, but there was plenty of blame to go around. The editors of the *Sun*, a young newspaper still trying to make its mark in Toronto, one of the most competitive media markets in North America, were derelict in their duties. They never checked Ramsay's work and they, too, got conned. Peter Desbarats, who was Dean of the School of Journalism at the University of Western Ontario when I was there, told Canada's *Maclean's* magazine that he thought the *Sun* editors had fallen into "a state of collective self-hypnosis. They desperately wanted the story to be true."

My father's exodus from newspapers was more than a professional blow. It was devastating to him, and the rest of his family. He was largely abandoned by his reporter friends, almost none of whom called or visited to help him through his humiliating ordeal in the weeks and months after he resigned. He went from journalistic celebrity to pariah overnight, it seemed, even though everyone knew that it was Ramsay, not him, who botched the Munro article. "He told me he never felt so lonely in his life, though he never complained about what happened to him," my mother said.

The premature end of Dad's career crushed me, too. I had just started my post-graduate degree in journalism. My father's scoops were the object of great admiration among other students. They wanted to know what it was like being the son of a famous reporter and whether I thought I could ever match his accomplishments. And then, several months into the program, my father's career was over. I was the object of pity, and my father a cautionary tale.

I never felt ashamed, and never felt that one mistake negated Dad's accomplishments as an investigative reporter and foreign correspondent. My student friends were good-hearted and tried to cheer me up, as did my journalism professors, most of whom had worked in newsrooms in the 1960s and 1970s, when Dad's career was at its peak. I will admit that his professional nightmare has haunted me for decades. Could the same thing happen to me? Sure, it could. I have long wondered if I would have been a more aggressive reporter, or spent more time as an investigative reporter, if his career had not come crashing down.

Dad put on a good face for his family, continued to function, and rarely talked about his pain. But depression cracked his normally cheery disposition. He ran out of money fast. My mother found low-paying retail jobs in eyewear and wine shops, even though, by then, her health was on the downswing.

Eventually Dad was appointed head of communications for the Ontario Ministry of Health, where a few of his ex-reporter friends worked and appreciated his writing skills. A couple of years after that, he became spokesman for the Ontario Ministry of Environment. They were good jobs that he found both stimulating and frustrating, given the stifling bureaucracy and silly jargon he had to endure. The highly politicized and hierarchal atmosphere of government was antithetical to the newsrooms in which he had worked. His plain speaking and opinionated manner often did him no favours in these roles.

After a heart attack in 1985, Dad underwent quadruple bypass heart surgery. He went back to his government job but tired easily and called it quits in 1986, declining the pension he was offered but did not think he deserved. He scrambled for freelance writing assignments, none of which paid well but they occasionally lifted his spirits. He wrote about the environment for various outlets, including *The Globe and Mail*. There were two or three times when he and I had bylines in the newspaper on the same day. He picked up a first-place award in 2006 from the Outdoor Writers of Canada association and two nominations from the National Magazine Awards.

Patrick Walsh, editor-in-chief of *Outdoor Canada* magazine, remembers my father pitching a story about the Ontario government's use of Agent

Orange, the cancer-causing defoliant used lavishly by the US military in Vietnam, in northern Ontario as late as 1972. Walsh passed. Sure enough, a year later, shortly after Dad's death, the story broke in the mainstream press. "Bob was right again. And well ahead of the pack," Walsh wrote in a remembrance of my father.

He also wrote about Slovak heritage in Canada for Slovak publications and was a board member of the Slovak Canadian Heritage Museum in Mississauga, Ontario. But mostly, he lived for his cottage in northwestern Ontario, his labour of love and gift to his wife, children, and three grandchildren. He turned down several requests from publishers to write his life story. Though flattered, I think he simply could not face the inevitable chapters about his journalistic collapse.

That pain never left him and I am afraid I made it worse. About two months after he lost his job, Dad and I were doing some carpentry work on the barn at the lakeside family cottage in northwestern Ontario. A neighbour strolled over to admire the repair job and asked me if I was proud of my father. "I was," I blurted out, and immediately realized I had made a huge mistake. I was not serious, of course. But I am prone to insensitive blurts that are meant to be funny, and sometimes are not. The two-word remark cut through Dad like a dagger. I could see it on his face. I apologized, told him what I said was not true. I suspected he only half believed me. I have thought about that incident every day since then and it makes me wince with pain and regret. If one of my daughters even half-jokingly said she was not proud of me, I would be crushed.

That was about forty years ago and I am now more than a decade older than he was when his newspaper career came tumbling down. I have had a great run, with careers in four countries, stints in TV and magazines, and a string of major and minor journalism awards. I am one of the few of my generation of reporters still in the game. But I am well aware that my job could end at any moment, given the newspaper industry's savage cutbacks after we responded too slowly to the threat from digital news sites and social media.

My father died just before newsrooms became electronic marvels whose web versions took precedence over the dead-tree editions. The way we covered the start of the COVID-19 pandemic in 2020 would have been completely alien to him even though, in his final years, email and Google were very much part of his life. He believed that journalism had to be face to face. He believed that journalists should live the story and that the best interviews were done in person, when the reporter could read the body language of the man or woman sitting opposite him and form a connection, perhaps friendly, perhaps hostile. He was a great advocate of the boozy lunch or dinner, a tradition now long gone although still (barely) alive when I was working for *The Times* of London in the 1990s; a vicious hangover would garner respect from colleagues. Copious amounts of alcohol got tongues wagging, Dad would tell me, and he could back it up with the story of the drunken government aide and his Munsinger scoop. Dad was such a believer in the journalistic power of booze that he arrived at interviews with Bob Dylan and Oscar-winning Hollywood star Joan Crawford with a bottle of fine rum. That was in the 1960s. Crawford sent Dad a handwritten thank-you note, still in family possession, for the article he wrote about her. Her note mentions the bottle.

As the Vietnam War was my father's greatest, long-running story, the pandemic was mine, but face-to-face interviews, never mind alcohol, were rarely part of the mix. In all of 2020, when I was largely confined to my prison-like home office in Rome, I did only half a dozen in-person interviews, most of them when I risked a spring road trip to northern Italy, where the European pandemic started in February. The rest were by phone, email, or video calls. I covered one of the biggest tragedies of the post-Second World War era and did not see a single body even though people were dying in alarming numbers in hospitals and care homes all around me in Rome. My father could not have imagined such detached journalism. Today, we journalists, to a great degree, are gathering news one step removed from the action, and our craft is not the better for it. The texture, the emotions, the tactile connections—all gone. They will come back once the pandemic vanishes, but not entirely, partly because publishers who control expense accounts know that sending reporters into the field can be costly; the price of a Zoom call is nothing.

The pandemic prevented me from returning to Vietnam to finish researching my father's 1967 odyssey. I used Google Earth and Skype and

Zoom interviews to try to fill in the holes, but the effort, while necessary and convenient, was mostly unsatisfying. It all felt so remote, so impersonal. I wanted to visit the spots my father had visited that fell off my 2018 itinerary. I wanted to soak up the surroundings, sense the smells, and talk to the locals who had experienced the war, as I had done in Plei Beng, where I felt certain that the old Montagnard man I met, the one who remembered the US Army airlift erasing his village from the map, had seen my father.

I could do none of that in 2020. For that reason, retracing Robert Reguly's Vietnam journey, the assignment that allowed me to walk in his footsteps and brought me closer to him than I had ever been before, will always remain incomplete, partly a romantic mystery to me. Maybe it is better that way. It keeps me thinking about Dad, trying to imagine the adventures, emotions, and sensations of a reporter who lived his war assignment to its roaring, bloody fullest. And it fills me with wonder, respect, and envy.

Today, I still see Dad's flaws, but the journey I took that began with retracing his footsteps in Vietnam helped me reclaim the admiration and respect I once had for him—and more. I learned that Dad was an extraordinarily brave truth warrior in service of the Fourth Estate. He had no interest in playing it safe as a "hotel journalist," as some of the more hesitant reporters of his era were called, even if he was well aware of the risks of going into battle armed with nothing more than a camera and a notebook. But I no longer think that being an action junkie defined him. In Vietnam, and in all his reporting, Dad did what he did, went where he went, because he wanted to find out what was really happening on the ground. Today, I remain in awe of his journalistic mission.

I will be forever envious of Dad's Vietnam assignment—I never have and never will get one like it. I am so proud of him for what he accomplished there. Following in his footsteps gave me a new level of respect not only for his sheer daring as a journalist, but for the humanity, intelligence, and foresight that infused his writing, and for the compassion for anyone he felt had been treated unjustly. No, he was never a great father even if he was generous and entertaining. He was always away. When he was home, he was absent too, obsessed with the next big story, buried in newspapers, drinking with contacts, largely oblivious to the needs of his stressed-out wife and three young kids.

For that, I forgive him. Call it hero worship. Because a hero he was, to me. Following his footsteps in Vietnam made me realize he was far more than a thrill seeker. He was a truth warrior, driven by astounding bravery.

ACKNOWLEDGEMENTS

WHEN THE GLOBE AND MAIL sent me to Vietnam in 2018 to retrace my father's footsteps as a war correspondent, fulfilling a life-long dream of mine, I never occurred to me that my journey would ultimately result in a book. Yet here it is, not just an expansion of the 9,000-word newspaper piece, but an entirely new endeavor, written during trying times—in a pandemic, when travel and working full-time as a foreign correspondent suddenly became a lot more complicated. I wouldn't call it fun; it was a labour of love.

The book is not entirely mine, of course. It would never have happened were it not for the support of The Globe, whose publisher and editors had the imagination to send me to Vietnam. It was an expensive gamble. Neither they, nor I, had any idea what I would find on the ground half a century after Robert Reguly covered the war for the Toronto Star. For taking that risk and encouraging me to go, I will be forever grateful to Globe publisher Phillip Crawley, editor-in-chief David Walmsley, his deputy Sinclair Stewart, and foreign editor Angela Murphy. Thank you all.

Writing Ghosts of War in one sense was a lonely endeavor. Most of it was bashed out in splendid isolation at a friend's 16th Century farmhouse in central Italy, where my only distraction was early morning bike rides in the mountains. In another sense, I was never truly alone because my freelance book editor, Carol King, was never more than a phone or video call away. Carol, a Briton who lives in Sicily, was alternately bluntly critical (exactly what I needed) or empathetic to the emotions churned up by my deep dive into my father's glamorous yet tortured career and difficult family life. She always asked the right questions and insisted on the right deletions and additions. Grazie, amica mia.

I am grateful to my wife, Karen Zagor, a UN speech writer and former journalist, who had faith in the project when mine waivered, and who also wielded the editing scalpel on my late drafts, deftly so. She knew my father well and was his cottage cribbage adversary, so hers too was a labour of love.

Nor was I alone in Vietnam. My fixer, Nhung Nguyen, a young journalist from Ho Chi Minh City, steered me across southern Vietnam, hunting for long-forgotten battle sites from which my father reported. Her charm, humour and grace—and killer smile—always took the edge of my anxiety. Since the Vietnam War is taught only in a rudimentary fashion in Vietnamese schools, our trip was a voyage of discovery for her, too.

I had plenty of help elsewhere. My deepest thanks to Astrid Lange, the Toronto Star's research librarian, who tracked down a small, precious array of my father's photos from Vietnam and a couple of other wars he covered. Some of those photos had migrated to the Toronto Reference Library, whose courteous staff uncovered a small treasure of musty old Robert Reguly shots for me on short notice. Thanks also to Michael Posner, one of the most elegant writers The Globe has ever employed. His rollicking, full-page obituary of my father, published in March, 2011, helped inspire me to tell my father's story.

This book spans several continents and many countries. Besides Vietnam, no spot was more important for my research than Washington DC, where my father was based when he covered the war, witnessed Bobby Kennedy's assassination and the civil rights and anti-war protests that gripped late 1960s America. In Washington, I am especially grateful to Kim McGettigan, a former neighbour and my oldest friend. Her vivid memories of the eccentric Canadian family that invaded their street in 1966 helped to make the Chevy Chase chapter come alive.

I thank Ted Gorsline, of Hamburg, Germany, and Rudy Bies, of Mississauga, Ontario, for their moral support and encouragement. They were two of only a small number of friends of my father who did not abandon him when his journalistic career came crashing down. For their loyalty and compassion, all the Regulys are grateful.

Finally, I owe thanks to Bob's granddaughters—Arianna, Emma and Genevieve—who also helped inspire me to write the book. I wish the three of you had known your mad, mercurial, brilliant grandfather better, but hope Ghosts of War brings him closer to you. I am glad you inherited his curiosity, generosity, and compassion for the downtrodden.

Rome, November 2021